HEALING
THE
INNER SELF

------------ ooo -----------

CLINICAL EXAMPLES
REVISED EDITION

BY

Melvin C. Fish, Ph. D.

HEALING

THE

INNER SELF

----------- ooo -----------

CLINICAL EXAMPLES
REVISED EDDITION

BY

Melvin C. Fish, Ph. D.

**Additional copies can be obtained by either
visiting us at www.DrMFish.com
or by phoning: (435) 865-0993**

CONTENTS

INTRODUCTION

Many people, after reading my book "Healing the Inner Self – From darkness Into Light", have requested more information. They want material that will provide guidelines and examples. This book is intended to satisfy that need. If you have not read my first book, I would highly recommend that you read it to get a better understanding of the material being presented here.

In this book I will make every effort to present the material in a manner that will provide you with a step-by-step approach to healing the inner self. Most people when getting started with this kind of work want an exact approach, and without a definite routine they are fearful to even start. This book will supply that definite routine. In actual practice, once one becomes familiar with this routine, most people will have a tendency to alter the approach somewhat to fit their personality.

As you start doing this work always keep in mind one very important fact; you can't hurt anyone. Don't be afraid of making a mistake.

The Lord Jesus Christ is referred to as the Savior, and Christians all over the world talk about Him and how He took upon Himself the sins of the world. Christ did not just ask for our sins. He said, "Cast your burdens upon me. I will suffer for you and you will not have to suffer any more."

We all have many burdens that have very little to do

with our own personal sins. Every experience of life leaves a residue. That residue is more than a memory. It is an energy that is either positive or negative. The negative residues are the burdens referred to by Christ when he said, "Cast your burdens upon me." We have problems associated with issues of the past such as abuse, rejection and neglect. These events from our past create burdens such as fear, anger, low self-esteem and guilt. All such burdens can be cast upon the Lord. The process is called "making the atonement work on a daily basis," and is really the process of "healing the inner self."

Sometimes we tend to cling to our burdens and it helps if we have a facilitator who can help us walk through the process of letting go. This process could be referred to as "spiritual alignment." As one aligns one's spirit with the Lord, one's thoughts, feelings and emotions are tuned into Him and the atonement becomes a reality.

Both this book and my previous book are entitled "Healing The Inner Self." The healing process referred to here is the healing of the spirit and is a process that takes place between you and the Lord Jesus Christ. I have never claimed to have healed anyone of anything. I am just a facilitator who helps one let go of their burdens and thus make the atonement a reality in one's life. The purpose of this book is to help you facilitate the healing of your own spirit and the spirit of others.

One may ask, what about people who do not believe in Jesus Christ? In such a case one should release their burdens by giving them to the God of their belief system. God is a kind loving Father and he judges one according to the intent of one's heart. I have worked with many non-Christians and have found the system to work equally well for them.

This book will be divided into four sections.

SECTION ONE: In the first section of this book I will present a suggested sequence dealing with the basic concepts and techniques to be used in the process of healing the inner self. This will be a generic presentation dealing with a fictitious person. The purpose of this presentation is to present general procedures for each step in the suggested sequence. It will help one when dealing with unresolved issues and problems, including problems and issues of both past and present. The techniques presented here will help one to release the stress and give the burden to Christ.

I suggest that as you start doing this work you should follow this sequence as closely as possible. This sequence will help you address all the important issues and steps of the process. As stated before, however, if you overlook one step or get things out of order, don't feel that you are going to hurt anyone. The worst thing that can happen is that nothing happens.

SECTION TWO: This will be a collection of actual real life examples. Examples can be of great worth.

They help us by opening our minds to new possibilities and procedures. It is true, however, that no two people are exactly alike and therefore no two problems are exactly alike. There are many similarities that can be very helpful.

This will be a collection of true experiences with real live people. Only the names have been changed or deleted to protect those whose stories are being told.

The following examples are given with the intent that they will help those who work as facilitators to assist others to heal their inner self, or when one is doing self-therapy. In either case, don't expect everything to proceed exactly as I have presented here, but rather let these examples be suggestions and then go by the guidance of the spirit. No two people are exactly alike and therefore each case will be unique.

SECTION THREE: This section includes material that is not in my first book. Some of it adds to and clarifies some of the steps in the suggested sequence. It is intended to be an extension or addition to that material. Some of the material in this section will include a number of additional concepts and helpful techniques that are not included in the suggested sequence. After going through the regular routine one may find some residual darkness that can be released with these techniques.

SECTION FOUR: Appendage

This section is a handy ready reference.

SECTION ONE

In this section I will begin by giving a suggested sequence. Then I will go through that sequence step by step.

It should be noted that in a typical session, because of the uniqueness of each individual, a facilitator should not expect to be able to follow the exact sequence every time. The approach will be very similar each time, but there will be some variation, especially when one learns to be guided by the spirit. If the spirit prompts you to change your approach, always follow the spirit.

Very seldom does one go through every one of the listed steps in a single session. We simply use the ones that the spirit wants used at that time.

I go through the suggested sequence step by step here because it is the best way I know to teach the techniques used in each step.

HEALING THE INNER SELF: SUGGESTED SEQUENCE

1.   Make sure the lie detector works. Introduce Kinesiology.

2.   Test for switching.

3.   Test each chakra making sure each one is open and flowing properly.

4.   Test for spirit attachments. If present, send them to the light.

5.   Test for spirits that may have come at the time of birth. If present, send them to the light. Then fill the void.

6.   Measure the stress level.

7.   Do an age regression to find an issue from the past. Release the issue. Repeat until no more issues from the past are found.

8.   Test for issues related to father, mother, brother, sister, extended family, neighbors, etc. Release when found.

9.	Test for issues related to fear, anger, abuse, rejection, etc. Release when found.

10.	Test for negative spiritual gifts. Release when found. Then fill the void.

11.	Test for fragmentation of the spirit involving fragments large enough to have a personality of their own. Do soul retrieval if needed.

12.	Test for fragmentation of the spirit involving small fragments without a personality of their own. Retrieve them if needed.

13.	Release fears and phobias as needed.

14.	Test for ritual abuse. Release as needed.

15.	Release the negative programming from the physical self.

Note: This is only a suggested sequence. Often the Holy Spirit will direct one to change the sequence. Unless the Holy Spirit directs otherwise, at least until you are totally familiar with the process, you will probably find your work to be most effective when you follow this sequence. As you work with these concepts feel free to add delete or change to fit your needs. No two people or situations are the same; therefore it is important that you allow the spirit to direct you as you work.

In actual practice, one often does not finish the entire sequence in one session. Sometimes that is too much for the client to handle all at once. Don't feel that you must finish the sequence. Go as far as you can then arrange to continue at another time.

To avoid unnecessary repetition I will here give a typical approach to each step in the suggested sequence. Later in section two where I give real live examples I will often refer back to this generic presentation instead of repeating tedious details. Each step in the suggested sequence will be followed, when necessary, with clarifying notes and suggestions.

The following is a generic example of a session involving a fictitious woman named Jane Nelson. She is married, and is thirty years of age. In this generic example I will refer to Jane by name, but in the real life examples that are given in the next section, to protect the identity of the client, I will only refer to them by their initials. In the following examples, and throughout the remainder of the book, "F" stands for the facilitator.

1

MAKE SURE THE LIE DETECTOR WORKS. INTRODUCE KINESIOLOGY

Because the facilitator sometimes works in person and sometimes by phone, I will present both approaches.

a. In this example the facilitator is working in person.

F.   "Jane, are you familiar with kinesiology-muscle testing?"

Jane.   "No."

F.   "Let me do a little demonstration." He has her hold her arm out level with the floor. He gives the command, "Hold" then applies steady but firm pressure to the wrist pushing straight downward. The arm seems to be locked firmly in place. He then makes a quick downward stroke along the midline of the front of the body with his hand. The hand does not come in contact with the body, but rather is kept about three to four inches away from the body. He again instructs Jane to hold her arm out as before and he repeats the command, "Hold," then once again he applies firm steady pressure as before. This time it easily drops downward.

Jane is surprised at how little strength she seems to have the second time. He strokes again as before only this time he strokes upward along the midline of the body. Again the command, "Hold," is given and firm steady pressure is applied. The arm seems to lock firmly in place.

F.   "The Chinese teach that there is an energy called Chi that flows up and down through channels in the body called Meridians. Every organ and muscle of the body is connected to one of these meridians. There is one meridian that flows up the midline of the front of the body. The muscle which holds the arm up is connected to that meridian."

"We all have an energy field that extends at least a foot or two out from the body, so I do not even have to touch you to have our energy fields interact. When I stroke either up or down in front of the body my energy field will interact with yours. When I stroke up it strengthens you, because that is the natural direction of the flow of your energy. When I stroke down, it weakens you."

"Your spirit has the ability to control the flow of that energy. By doing so the spirit can give us coded messages. This makes it possible for us to bypass the conscious mind and communicate directly with your spirit. This is the way it will work: When I ask a question, you

10

will answer. If your spirit agrees with the answer, it will stimulate the flow of your energy and your arm will lock in place. If your spirit does not agree with the answer given, it will turn that energy off and the arm will unlock.

Once one understands how the system works, it becomes quite obvious that kinesiology is really scientific.

Let us now test the system to make sure it works. Answer 'yes.' Is your name Jane?"

Jane.   "Yes."

The facilitator commands "Hold," then applies firm steady pressure to the arm and it locks firmly in place.

F.   "Jane, your spirit agreed with the answer. Now Jane, answer no. Is your name Jane?"

Jane.   "No."

The facilitator again commands "hold," and applies firm steady pressure to the arm. The arm goes down easily.

F.   "Your spirit disagreed with your answer. Your lie detector works perfectly."

Note: It has been demonstrated that the system works and the session can proceed to the next step.

Note 1: Always when the facilitator tests he first commands, "hold," and then applies firm steady pressure to the arm. It is important that the command, "hold," is given before the pressure is applied. It doesn't matter whether the client answers "yes" or "no." In either case, if the arm is locked the answer given is true, and if the arm unlocks the answer given is false.

Note 2: In the examples of actual sessions that follow I will not repeat all these details, but rather, I will indicate that the facilitator introduced kinesiology and found that the spirit of the client was communicating properly.

b. In this example the facilitator is working by phone.

Because there is no personal physical contact while doing the testing, the testing must be conducted by means of a surrogate. The facilitator tests by using his fingers, and thus he becomes the surrogate. The thumb and first finger of each hand are pressed together firmly and the thumb and finger of one hand are interlocked with the thumb and finger of the other hand. After asking a question, and an answer has been given, he tugs as if trying to pull his hands apart. When the spirit agrees with the answer, the fingers remain locked together. If the spirit disagrees with the answer the fingers easily separate, allowing the hands to pull apart.

An alternate way to do the test is to press the thumb and the first finger of the left hand (if you are right handed) together tightly forming a circle. The index finger of the right hand is inserted into that circle. After the question has been given and the answer received the facilitater then makes a sharp forward motion with the finger of the right hand trying to force it to break the circle by separating the thumb and index finger. When the spirit agrees with the answer given the fingers will remain tightly together. When the spirit disagrees with the answer given the finger of the right hand will easily break the circle.

Sometimes when working in person, for some reason, it may be desirable that the facilitator makes no physical contact with the client. In such cases this surrogate approach to testing can be used very effectively.

F.   " Jane, are you familiar with kinesiology muscle testing?"

Jane.   "No."

F.   "There is an energy which the Chinese call Chi. This energy flows up and down through channels in the body called meridians. Each organ and each muscle of the body is connected to a meridian. If the flow of energy is strong the muscle, when tested, will be strong. If the flow of energy is weak, the muscle, when tested, will be weak. A person's spirit can control the flow of that energy and by doing so it can give a coded message."

"The spirit will either agree or disagree when an answer is given. If the spirit agrees with an answer it will stimulate the flow of energy and the muscle that is being tested will be strong. If the spirit disagrees with the answer, it will turn the energy off and the muscle, when tested, will be weak."

"Spirits communicate through thought transfer and distance does not interfere with that communication process. I would like to ask questions and have your spirit communicate to my spirit whether or not it agrees with the answer you give. Through the use of kinesiology, my spirit will in turn communicate the answer to me. In that way we can bypass your conscious mind and communicate directly with your spirit. In this way we can get answers that we could not get in other ways. Does this make sense?"

Jane. "Yes."

F.   "I need to begin by making sure that our spirits are communicating properly. I am directing this question to your spirit. I need you to answer, 'Yes.' Do I have permission to communicate directly with you, spirit to spirit, through thought transfer?"

Jane. "Yes."

The facilitator tests, and his fingers remain locked indicating that the answer is yes.

F.   "We seem to be communicating.   My spirit indicated that your answer was 'yes.'   Now, please again answer 'yes' to this question. Is your name Jane?"

Jane. "Yes."

The facilitator tests and gets a firm response.

F.   "Now say no."

Jane. "No."

The facilitator tests and gets a very weak response.

Note: The system is working and the session is ready to proceed to the next step.

Note;   In most sessions, the client does not understand kinesiology and there must be a short teaching session as given here; however, in the examples of actual sessions that follow I will not repeat all these details. I will indicate that the facilitator introduced kinesiology and found that the client's spirit was communicating properly. Also, throughout the remainder of this book I will not give a detailed description of how the question is given and the answer tested. I will simply state (test, yes) to indicate that the kinesiology test indicated that the answer was yes. And (test, no) will indicate that the answer was no.

As previously stated, the surrogate test, or self-testing as described above can be used when working with someone in person, but there are some advantages in testing by using the client's arm. The use of the client's arm seems to increase the client's level of belief in the process. It also helps the client have a higher level of trust and belief in the facilitator.

2

TESTS FOR SWITCHING

Sometimes as you go through all the procedures of step one above, you still can not get a strong "yes" or a weak "no." This is often due to a condition called "being switched." Being switched will also affect the accuracy of the answers you are receiving.

There is an easy way to test for being switched and it only takes a minute. To make sure you are getting good accurate answers this test should be conducted at this time.

To test for the condition of being switched one first needs to understand a little about two of the meridians of energy in the human body and how they interact.

There is a meridian of energy called "Central." This meridian begins at the middle of the pubic bone. The energy flows up the midline of the body ending at the middle of the lower lip. This is the meridian you were manipulating at the beginning of step one above. You were temporarily strengthening and weakening that meridian when you stroked up and down in front of the body.

To test the central meridian, the arm of the client is extended down and out so as to make a 30-degree angle with the body. The elbow is kept straight. The arm is in a position that is half way between being extended to the

17

front and to the side. When testing, the arm is pushed in a direction that would bring the hand into the groin. To test simply command, "Hold," then apply firm steady pressure in the indicated direction. If the energy is flowing properly, the arm will lock in place.

There is another meridian called "Governing." This one starts at the tailbone. The energy flows up the midline of the back, over the head, down the middle of the face and ends at the middle of the upper lip.

To test the Governing meridian the client bends the elbow and places the tips of the fingers at the small of the back. The elbow should point directly to the side. When testing, the direction of motion is for the arm to rotate so that the elbow is moving toward the front of the body. Of course the arm cannot rotate very far. The facilitator places one hand on the shoulder on the same side as the arm that is being tested. This is done to stabilize the body. The other hand is placed behind the elbow. A command, "Hold," is given and the elbow is pulled or pushed toward the front of the body. If the energy in that meridian is flowing properly the arm will lock in place.

To test for switching all that is necessary is to test the Central meridian, then the Governing meridian, then immediately test Central again. If all three tests give a firm response there is no problem. If there is a problem it will show up as follows: Test Central, (firm response). Test Governing, (firm response). Test Central again, (weak response).

What happens when one is switched is that when Governing is tested immediately after testing Central, Governing will steal energy from Central so that the second time you test Central there is a lack of energy and you will get a weak test.

To correct the problem, all that is needed is to "run Governing backward about five times and put the energy into Central". This is done by placing your hand near the client's upper lip and running the hand up over the head and down the back, keeping the hand three to four inches away from the body. By doing this, you are running the meridian backward, and by doing so, energy is drained out of the Governing meridian. Immediately test Central again. This tells the body where to put that energy. The energy goes into the Central meridian balancing the system. This should completely correct the problem and make it easier to get good communication with the client's spirit when doing the kinesiology testing.

In a very small percentage of cases a client may be switched in the opposite mode. By that I mean the out of balance condition is created by having Central steal energy from Governing instead of the other way around as described above. In this case the testing will go as follows: Test Governing, (firm response). Test Central, (firm response). Test Governing again, (weak response). Governing is weak the second time because Central has stolen energy from Governing.

To correct this problem "run Central backward

about five times and put the energy into Governing." This is done by starting at the lower lip of the client and stroking down the front of the body. Keep the hand about three to four inches from the body. Do this about five times then immediately test Governing. This will drain the excess energy out of Central and put it back into Governing where it belongs.

3

TEST EACH CHAKRA MAKING SURE EACH ONE IS OPEN AND FLOWING PROPERLY.

According to Oriental medicine, there is spiritual energy known as Chi which enters the body through entry points known as chakras. There are seven of them. Each one is a whirlpool of energy entering the body. This energy flows up and down the body through channels known as meridians. The basic concept of Oriental medicine is that by balancing that energy, the body can heal itself.

If any of the chakras are not open or flowing properly, a person's health and strength can be seriously impaired. I once worked with a woman who did not have the strength to move a hand. She could not even turn her head or move her foot. It was found that her chakras were almost completely closed with very little Chi energy entering her body. Once the chakras were opened her normal energy immediately returned.

The chakras are numbered from the bottom up. All of them are located along the midline of the body except for the heart chakra, which is located slightly to the left of the midline. Chakra number one is located at the tip of the tailbone. Number two is about half way between the pubic bone and the navel. Number three is in the pit of the stomach half way between the navel and the ribcage. Number four, the heart chakra, enters the heart slightly to the left of the midline. Number five, known as the throat chakra, enters the throat at the point of the larynx. Number six, the third eye chakra, enters the forehead slightly above the level of the eyebrows. Number seven, the crown chakra, enters the top of the head.

Each of the chakras numbered two through six is really a pairs of chakras. Each one has a second branch that enters the back of the body about an inch below the front entry point.

The facilitator tests each chakra to make sure it is open and flowing properly. This is done by hold one hand of the facilitator over the chakra being tested, while using his/her other hand to do a kinesiology test, testing one of the client's arms.   If the chakra is open and flowing properly the arm will give a very firm test; if not, there will be a very weak test. The most natural way to test is to go in order from top to bottom, testing the front branch of each chakra.

If any chakra, when tested, results in a weak test, correct the problem before proceeding to the next chakra. The correction is begun by having the facilitator place one hand near the body but not touching it. It is to be placed over the chakra. It is then rotated or swirled around over the chakra. This can be either clockwise or counter clockwise. Test the client while asking, "Is this the proper direction of rotation for this chakra?" Some chakras rotate clockwise and some rotate counter-clockwise. It will vary from person to person so it is important to test to find out which way the chakra rotates.

After determining the correct direction of rotation, swirl the chakra several times. Then reach in toward the body with both hands, fingers spread apart, and pull the hand away from the body as if combing the chakra. Comb the chakra several times. Again swirl and comb, swirl and comb several times. Do the same technique over the back branch of the chackra. Then test again by holding your hand over the chakra while doing the kinesiology test as before. Once you get a good strong test proceed to the next chakra.

The facilitator is now ready to proceed to the next step.

4

TEST FOR SPIRIT ATTACHMENTS. IF PRESENT, SEND THEM TO THE LIGHT.

F.   "Jane, I would like to test some of your basic energy fields. May I do that?"

Jane. "Yes."

The facilitator cups his hand behind her neck; then with the other hand he does a kinesiology test by applying pressure to one of her wrists. Jane extends her arm to be tested. He commands, "Hold," and then tests. The test is strong.   If the test had given a weak response, it would have indicated the presence of spirits. It is important to note that a strong test does not guarantee that one is free from spirit attachments. Sometimes the spirits can hide. For that reason the Lord has provided us with two other ways to test.

There is a second test. The facilitator performs this test by cupping one hand and placing it gently over Jane's forehead, and at the same time, with his other hand, he tests one of Jane's arms. This time there is a strong response. This indicates the presence of spirits.

A weak test would have indicated the possibility of being free from spirit attachments. Again, there is no guarantee of being clear. Sometimes the spirits can hide, but we try every way possible to find them. There is a third test. That one is to just ask, "Do you have any foreign spirits of any kind attached to you in any way?" The client answers either "Yes" or "No." Follow the question with a kinesiology test.

It is important to note that the responses of the first two tests are reversed. When holding the back of the neck, a <u>weak test</u> indicates the presence of spirits. When holding the forehead, a <u>strong test</u> indicates the presence of a spirit.

The facilitator places one hand on Jane's shoulder. He then repeatedly does a kinesiology test asking, "How many? One, hold." (Test, strong.) "Two, hold." (Test, strong.) "Three hold." (Test, weak)

F.   "Jane, let me explain what I was testing. In the Bible, it is interesting to note that with half of the people Jesus Christ healed, all he did was to get rid of spirits that were attached to the sick person. We often have spirits dwelling within us or attached to us. This does not have anything to do with whether one is good or bad. Like any physical problem, it just is. The test I just did with you indicated that you have at least three spirits in some way connected to you. In such a situation people often describe the situation by saying, 'you are possessed by a spirit.' I do not like that term because it implies that the spirits are controlling you. There are extreme cases where the spirit is in control, but in most cases the influence is very subtle." Even though the influence seems to be very subtle, these spirits can have a tremendous effect upon our health and our mood.

"There are two types of spirits that often attach themselves to living mortals. In scripture they are referred to as devils and unclean spirits. The devils are the ones who followed Satan, and who have never had a body of their own. The unclean spirits are the spirits of people who have lived and died, and have remained earthbound. I would like to find out what kind of spirits are here with you."

F.   Using kinesiology, "Jane, are any of the spirits who are here with you the kind we call a devil?" (Test, yes).

F.   "Are any of the spirits who are with you the kind we would call unclean, meaning that they have previously had a mortal body of their own?" (Test, yes).

"We now know that both kinds of spirits are present. It will be necessary to deal with them separately."

F.   "I would like to talk to the spirits that we refer to as devils."

"You are here, hiding from Satan. You really don't

want to go back to him for a new assignment because no matter how hard you try to please him, he always punishes and says, 'not good enough.' He controls through fear. You hate him but you feel trapped."

"I am here to set you free. You have been controlled by Satan so long that you have forgotten who you really are. You are literally a child of God, and Jesus Christ is your brother. They both love you very much and are anxious for you to realize that you have been deceived. They both want you to come back to them."

"All you need to do is to cry out to Christ and say, 'I was deceived. Please forgive me. I want to come back and be with you.'"

"Christ will heal and cleanse you. You will have your light and glory restored and become the great entity of light and power that you once were. You are free to go now. Please turn to Christ and go to the light"

"Jane, I am going to test again. Please answer yes."

"Jane, are there any devils within you or attached to you in any way?" (Test, no).

F.   "The devils are gone. Do you feel any different?"

Jane.   "Yes. It is hard to explain. I guess I would just say that I feel lighter."

F.   "The remaining spirits, are the ones who have lived as mortals upon the earth and have died. These spirits are earthbound. They see us and interact with us even though we do not see them. I will now talk to them"

"We are all children of God, and are therefore members of the God race. As children of God we have the power to create. This is the way it works. What one vividly visualizes or thinks about with emotion is created. As we mortals think about something with emotion, our thoughts create something known as thought forms. These creations exist in the spirit realm. They hang around waiting to manifest in the physical dimension. It may take quite a long time before they manifest physically. For that reason we mortals usually do not connect our thoughts with that manifestation."

"When you died, crossing over into the realm of spirit, if you focused on thoughts and emotions such as guilt, anger, a desire for revenge, the negative way in which you died, or any other intensely negative thought, your thoughts and emotions created negative thought forms that are right there in the spirit realm with you. So, for you there is no time lapse between the creation of the thought form and its manifestation in the realm where you reside. In other words, you are creating a never-ending, ever-repeating nightmare of the worst events of your earthly life. It is time to set yourself free."

"Jesus Christ is the savior of all mankind. He has said, 'Cast your burdens upon me. I will suffer for you and you will not have to suffer any more.'"

"Turn to Christ and ask him to take your fear, your

anger, your guilt, or whatever negative thought you have been dwelling upon. He will remove that negativity from you, replacing the darkness with light."

"Look up. There are loved ones and friends hovering over you. They have been with you all along, but you were so focused on the negative aspects of your life that you did not see them. They are here to take you to a better place. You are now free to go. Please go to the light."

At this point the facilitator tests to see if there are any spirits remaining with Jane. Using the same test as before, he holds the back of her neck with one hand while testing with the other. He commands, "hold," then applies steady firm pressure to the wrist. The arm is strong. He next tests while holding the forehead with one hand. He commands, "hold" and tests. This time the test is weak.

Both of these tests seem to indicate that Jane is clear.

F.   "Jane, those two tests seemed to indicate that the spirits are gone. I want to do one more test to make sure they are gone. Please answer 'yes'. Jane, are there any devils, unclean spirits, or any negative entities of any kind with you now?" (Test, yes).

At this point it was evident that there was still at least one spirit that did not go to the light when given the opportunity.

F.   "Jane, there is still at least one spirit with you. I would like to talk directly to that spirit. I will ask that spirit questions and you will answer just as you did before."

"I am talking to the spirit that is with Jane. You have darkness within you that has kept you earthbound. Does that darkness seem to have a mind of its own?" (Test, yes). (I am still talking to the spirit.) When you lived as a mortal you had a spirit hiding within you. That spirit is still there and in the same way it may have another spirit hiding within it. In fact there seems to be a nest of spirits that could involve any number of spirits."

"I am talking to all the spirits in the nest. It is time for each of you to be set free. Let me speak directly to the innermost spirit. I believe that you are one who followed Satan in the beginning. You are tired of his lies and his control. In fact you hate him and you are hiding from him. Is that true?" (Test, yes.)

"You do not need to hide from him any more. Just as I told the others, you are a child of God and Jesus Christ is your brother. They love you very much. They know that you were deceived, but they do not hold that against you. If you will cry out to Christ and say, 'I was deceived. Please forgive me.' You will be cleansed of all the dark negative energy, thoughts, and emotions. You will have your light and glory returned, and you will be taken back into the light. Satan cannot go there. You will be free from him. You can go now."

"Now I am talking to the other spirits in the nest. As soon as the spirits who have been hiding within you are gone, all you need to deal with is your own problems. You can now do as the others did. Give your burdens to Christ and go to the light. All of you can go now. Please go to the light."

At this time all three tests indicate that all the spirits are gone.

Sometimes when testing the facilitator will have the client answer "yes" then test, then ask the same question with the client answering "no." For example, in the above case The facilitator tested by asking if there were any spirits present. She answered "yes" and the arm was weak, meaning the answer was no. Then as a double check she answered "no" and the arm was strong, meaning that again the answer was no.

F. "As far as your spirit knows, at this time there are no negative spirits with you. We do need to dig just a little deeper though. (At this point we move on to step five.)

Note 1: Testing for spirits is one of the most important steps in the entire session. For that reason I will restate the procedure to make sure there is no misunderstanding.

The way to test for spirit attachments is to hold one hand behind the neck. Cup the hand and hold the neck gently. While holding the neck use the other hand to do a kinesiology test on one of the clients arms. The arm should remain firmly locked in place. If there is a weak response, there is a spirit present. You can count the number of spirits that are present by saying, "How many? One, hold." (Test) "Two, hold." (Test) "Three, hold." (Test) etc. Continue until you get a weak response. For example, if on the count of one, two, and three the response is firm, then on four the response is weak, the number of spirits present would be at least four. Sometimes a spirit can hide. In which case the test may not reveal the presence of any spirits. Also, there may be more spirits present than were counted. For that reason it is important that there be additional ways of testing.

The second way to test for the presence of spirits is to cup the hand and gently hold the forehead of the client while doing a kinesiology test with the other hand. This time the result is just the opposite of the other. A weak test indicates the possibility of being clear. A firm test indicates the presence of spirits. Just as before, the number of spirits present can be counted.

A third way to test is to just ask, "I am talking to your spirit. Please take inventory of every aspect of the client including the spirit, the physical body, the mind, the intellect, and the energy fields. Are there any devils, unclean spirits, or foreign entities of any kind present?" The client answers, "Yes." You command, "hold" then test. In this case a strong test would indicate the presence of spirits. A weak test would indicate that there are none.

Again the number of such spirits can be counted.

The way to rid a client of the spirits is to send them to the light. Inasmuch as the devils and the unclean spirits fit into two completely different categories, they must be dealt with separately. It does not matter which one you deal with first. In either case, your objective is to help the spirit understand where he is and why, and to convince the spirit that it is not necessary to stay in that condition of hell or spirit prison where it is at the present time.

Sometimes it takes considerable talking and logic to convince the devils that they can and should go to the light. Please refer to the Appendage at the back of the book. There is a section entitled "Logic For Devils."

Note 2: In the true examples that follow I will not always give full details as given in this generic example. In cases where the spirits leave without much trouble, as in the above example, I will only say that the spirits were found and sent to the light. In more difficult cases, more details will be given.

Some people have difficulty dealing with the concept of spirit attachments. Many do not believe that the problem is real. For that reason I have included a page in the appendage entitled "Casting Our Devils." The quotations given there teach that the problem is real and should be dealt with.

Note 3: Sometimes a spirit can hide in such a way

that none of the three tests reveal their presence. When a person has a health problem dealing with a specific organ of the body, this is often the case. For example, a woman had been deaf in one ear for about ten years. All three tests failed to reveal the presence of any spirits. She was asked, "Is there a spirit hiding in your deaf ear?" The answer was yes, and when the spirit was sent to the light, the hearing immediately returned to normal.

If the client has a health problem involving a specific organ of the body, the facilitator should ask with kinesiology whether or not there are any spirits hiding in that particular organ.

5

TEST FOR SPIRITS THAT MAY HAVE COME AT THE TIME OF BIRTH. IF PRESENT, SEND THEM TO THE LIGHT, THEN FILL THE VOID.

F.   "Jane, it is possible for a spirit to enter at or near the time of birth. Some people have a hard time with that concept because they believe that 'Satan can have no power over one until one reaches the age of accountability.' The scripture only says that Satan cannot tempt you until you are accountable. It does not say that he can't influence an infant. He can and he does."

"When a spirit enters at or near the time of birth, one tends to accept that spirit along with the new body as an addition to oneself. Instead of recognizing it as a foreign entity, it is perceived to be a package of spiritual gifts. One will therefore bond to it and try to integrate it into one's soul."

"Jane, now that I have explained the concept, I need to ask your spirit another question. Answer, "yes."

"Are there any negative or foreign entities of any kind, who came at the time of birth, attached to you in any way?" (Test, yes)

"How many? One, hold." (Test, strong). "Two, hold." (Test, strong). "Three, hold." (Test, strong). "Four, hold." (Test, weak)."

"Jane, there are four spirits that have been with you from the time you were born. Usually such spirits are well meaning ones. They are trying to live your life along with you and they think that they are helping and contributing in some way. The truth is, they have darkness within them. This darkness keeps them earthbound, and that darkness has a negative effect upon you. It is time to send these spirits to the light."

"Jane, please repeat out loud after me."

Jane. She speaks to the spirits, repeating the following after the facilitator.

"Now that I know that you are not a part of me, I apologize for clinging to you and bonding to you. I release you. You are free to go to the light just as the others did. Please go to the light."

F.   While testing with kinesiology the facilitator asks, "are there any spirits who came at or near the time of birth still with you?" (Test, no). "They are all gone."

"Now that all of the spirits are gone, there is a void that must be filled. We all know that nature abhors a vacuum, so it is important that we fill it. We have the power to fill it with good positive things."

"The Orientals who have studied spiritual energy for two thousand years have found that when one raises one's arm to the square, as when one takes an oath, the arm acts as an antenna to draw spiritual energy, increasing and magnifying the power of the spoken words. At this time we need that extra spiritual energy. If you would, please, raise your arm to the square and repeat after me."

Jane. (She repeats) **"In the name of Jesus Christ I petition my Heavenly Father. Please fill the void within me by giving me at this time every positive spirit gift, intelligence, light, and anything I need to help me accomplish my life's mission."**

F. "Now do the following and I will explain later. Tap your chest in the middle about two inches below your collarbone while you say, 'accept,' (tap), 'accept,' (tap), 'accept,' (tap). Then hold your navel with the palm of your hand and say, 'forever with me.'"

"You were tapping above your thymus gland which produces white blood cells to help your body heal from disease. You have a spiritual thymus, which helps you heal spiritually. You just stimulated that spiritual thymus. You also brought positive energy in through your spiritual navel which also strengthened your spirit."

Note: Sometimes a person will cling to a spirit and will need some extra encouragement to let it go. The spirit has become part of their "comfort zone" and change can be painful. In such a case I like to tell the following true experience.

I once had a woman that came to me who was a professional musician. She played the guitar and sang. She had a spirit with her who, apparently during her life upon earth, was also a musician. This spirit really believed that she was the source of this woman's musical talent. The woman was afraid to let the spirit go for fear that she would lose her musical talent. Finally after about five months she came back to me.

She said, "I have decided that I have to be me. I can't go through life living on someone else's talent. Even if I lose my talent I have to be me."

She released the spirit and we sent the spirit to the light. About three weeks later she called and said, "You wouldn't believe what has happened to my talent. In the last three weeks it has blossomed way beyond anything I could do before. I now know that even though the spirit that was with me had good intentions, all she did was hold me back."

6

MEASURE THE STRESS LEVEL.

F.   Addressing Jane, "as one progresses through life, every experience leaves a residue of energy. That energy can be either positive or negative. That negative energy is the burden for which Christ asked when he said, 'Cast your burdens upon me. I will suffer for you, and you will not need to suffer anymore.'"

"I would like to help you find some of those issues and burdens of the past, then help you release them, giving the burden to Christ."

"So that we can measure our success, I would like to measure the amount of that negative energy you have accumulated during your life. We will measure it on a scale of zero to one hundred. At zero there is no stress or negative energy from the past. At one hundred you would self destruct because you could not endure any more negative energy."

"I will go through the numbers while testing with kinesiology. You need not respond verbally. Your spirit will let us know your stress level. It will do this by unlocking your arm when testing the number, or block of numbers that includes the number, that measures the negative energy and stress."

"Zero, hold." (Test, strong). "Zero to twenty, hold." (Test, strong). "Twenty to forty, hold." (Test, strong). "Forty to sixty, Hold." (Test, strong). "Sixty to eighty, hold." (Test, weak). "Sixty to seventy, hold." (Test, weak). "Sixty to sixty five, hold." (Test, strong). "Sixty-five, hold." (Test, strong). "Sixty-six, hold." (Test, strong). "Sixty-seven, hold." (Test, weak). "Your spirit has indicated that as perceived by the spirit, the stress level is at sixty-seven."

"We are now ready to look for the source of that stress."

Note: In the true examples that follow I will not give these same tedious details. For a stress test like the above example I would only indicate that a stress test showed that the stress level was sixty-seven.

7.

DO AN AGE REGRESSION TO FIND AN ISSUE FROM THE PAST. RELEASE THE ISSUE. REPEAT UNTIL NO MORE ISSUES FROM THE PAST ARE FOUND.

F.   "We will now do what is called an age regression. I will start at present age and count back through the years. When I come to an age at which time something happened that your spirit wants to release first, the arm will unlock. I cannot dig out anything from the past unless you and your spirit are ready to release it. You are in control."

"Jane, examine the years from present back to age twenty. Hold." (Test, strong). "Twenty to ten, hold." (Test, strong). "Ten to five, hold." (Test, weak). "This test indicated that something happencd between the ages of five and ten."

"Do you have any memory of anything stressful happening during that five year span of time?"

Jane.   "When I was about eight years old my family went to visit an aunt and uncle. They had four boys. One of them, George, was about twelve or thirteen. I don't know exactly what happened, but I have had some flashbacks that make me feel that something bad happened. I have never felt comfortable when I have been around George."

F.   While testing with kinesiology he asks, "Think about George. Hold." (Test, weak). "Think about fear. Hold." (Test, strong). " Think about abuse. Hold." (Test, weak). "Think about sexual abuse. Hold." (Test, weak).

"It seems as if some form of sexual abuse occurred at that time. How do you feel about that?"

Jane. "I have always thought that there was some sexual abuse, but I could never say for sure. This confirms my feelings and explains why I never felt comfortable when I was with him."

F.   "Are you ready to forgive and let go of the past?"

Jane. "How can I forgive a person who has abused me and brought negativity into my life? I feel that he has damaged me. I will never be the same. I don't think I am ready to forgive."

F.   "When you forgive someone for an offense toward you, that does not take him off the hook. In other words, you do not in any way release him from his responsibility. He is still accountable for what he has done."

"When you forgive him, what you do is take yourself off the hook. In other words, by forgiving him you release yourself from the negative energy and emotion that binds you to that negative event."

"Jane, let me ask again. Are you ready to forgive and let go of the past?"

Jane. "Yes."

F. "As I walk you through the process of letting go of that issue, I will use the word love. I do not mean romantic love. I mean Christ-like love."

"Get a picture of George in your mind. Imagine that he is here with you. How do you feel?"

Jane. "I feel afraid, and angry."

F. "As you look at George, in your mind, tell him, **'the past is over. It doesn't matter any more except for what we can learn from it. I love you and want you to heal. I offer to you all the healing that is available through Christ. I forgive you for everything you said or did that offended me in any way. I forgive you for the things that you did not say or did not do that offended me. Please forgive me for anything that offended you. I love you.'"**

She follows along repeating the above, and then there is a little pause while she processes this silently in her mind. She gives the facilitator a signal to indicate that she has finished. He then continues.

F.   "Jane, please repeat that again in your mind. To do this get a picture of George in your mind, then <u>in your own words</u> tell him: The past is over. It does not matter except for what we can learn. I love you. I forgive you. Forgive me. I love you."

Again there is a short pause, and then she indicates that she has finished.

F.   "Imagine that you can look within yourself, and you see a dark cloud of negative energy there. This is the energy associated with the sexual abuse. Take several deep breaths. As you inhale, imagine that you are inhaling light. As you exhale, imagine that you are exhaling that darkness. Tell me when you feel that the darkness is gone."

Jane.   After several deep breaths, "I feel better now."

F.   "Get a picture of George in your mind. Imagine that he is here now." The facilitator commands, " Hold," then tests. The test is strong. This indicates that the stress is gone. He double checks by asking, "What do you feel now when you think of him?"

Jane.   "All I feel is love. He really is a good person."

At this point the facilitator makes a mental note. There is a strong possibility that there is a fragmentation of the spirit. It will be important that this is checked later and if it is the case, integrate those fragments back into the spirit. The facilitator should make sure that before the session is ended, that there is a test for fragmentation of the spirit.

The facilitator does another age regression, but nothing else comes up so the session is ready to proceed to the next step.

8

TEST FOR ISSUES RELATED TO FATHER, MOTHER, BROTHER, SISTER, EXTENDED FAMILY, NEIGHBORS, ETC. RELEASE WHEN FOUND.

F.   While testing he asks, "Think about your mother. Hold." (Test, strong). "Think about your father. Hold." (Test, weak).

"There seems to be an issue with your father. Tell me about your father."

Jane.   "My mother and father divorced when I was five. Up until that time I had a very close relationship with my father. After the divorce I felt rejected by him."

F.   "Do you have any contact with him now?"

Jane.   "Yes. I see him quite often but it is not as close a relationship as I would like."

F.   "Think about the divorce of your parents. Hold." (Test, weak). "Think of the word, rejection. Hold." (Test, weak)."

"There really is an issue with rejection. Get a picture of your father in your mind, and think about the divorce. Now, just as you did with George, in your own words tell your father, **'the past is over. It does not matter except for what we can learn from it. I love you. I forgive you for anything you said or did that offended me. Please forgive me for anything that offended you. I love you'**"

There is a pause, and then she indicates that she is finished.

F.   "Jane, please go through that again; only first imagine that there is a bright beam of light connecting your heart to his. That beam of light is a positive bond that connects you to your father."

After a short pause she indicates that she has finished the visualization. Another test shows that the negative feelings toward her father are gone and that she is now bonded to him. No issues involving other people come up, so we go on to the next step.

Note: The fact that Jane had an issue with rejection indicates that there is a strong possibility that there is a negative gift of rejection. It is important that the facilitator makes a mental note of this and makes sure that that possibility is dealt with before the session is ended.

TEST FOR ISSUES RELATED TO FEAR, ANGER, ABUSE, REJECTION, ETC.   RELEASE WHEN FOUND.

F.   Continuing testing.   "Think of the word fear. Hold." (Test, strong).   "Anger, Hold." (Test, strong). "Abuse, Hold." (Test, strong). "Rejection, Hold." (Test, weak)."

"Jane, we released the feeling of rejection that came from having your parents divorce. Because rejection came up again, it seems as if there is someone else who has made you feel rejected. Do you have any idea who it would be?"

Jane. "Yes, I think it would be my husband. His work takes him away from home a lot. I know that it is necessary but still, I hate it."

At this point Jane is taken through the same process with her husband that she went through with George, and with her father. A follow up test shows that the stress has been released.

TEST FOR NEGATIVE SPIRITUAL GIFTS. RELEASE WHEN FOUND, THEN FILL THE VOID.

F.   "Do you believe in gifts of the spirit?"

Jane. "Yes."

F.   "Do you believe that there is opposition in all things?"

Jane. "Yes."

F.   "Everything must have an opposite. Both scripture and science agree on this principle. If something had no opposite, it would cease to exist. Because there is opposition in all things, both the Holy Spirit and Satan can give you spiritual gifts. When the Holy Spirit gives you a spiritual gift it increases your ability to perform in a positive way. When Satan gives you a spiritual gift it increases your ability and potential to perform in a negative way. Let us look for some of those negative gifts."

At this point the facilitator uses kinesiology to test key words that could be the name of negative spiritual gifts. These words include words such as: fear, fear of failure, fear of success, anger, guilt, rejection, low self-esteem, doubt, control, resentment, hate, etc.

The Facilitator tests for the gift of guilt by saying, "Do you have a gift of guilt? (Test, yes.) In this manner, several other gifts were found these included fear and low self-esteem. These gifts probably came as a result of the sexual abuse. Rejection also produced a weak test. This gift probably came because of feeling rejected by both her father and her husband.

F.   "Would you like to get rid of those negative spiritual gifts?"

Jane.   "Yes, I surely would. I have been dealing with these issues for as long as I can remember."

F.   "To do that we need a little extra spiritual energy, so raise your arm to the square and repeat after me."

Jane.   (She repeats.) **"In the name of Jesus Christ I command that all negative spiritual gifts depart. I dismiss them without argument and cancel them out along with every spirit, thought form, energy, and residue associated with them. Cancel, (tap). Cancel, (tap). Cancel, (tap). Forever cancel."**

As she says, "cancel," she taps the chest over the thymus, which is in the middle of the chest about two inches below the collarbone. While saying, "For ever cancel" she holds her navel with the palm of one hand.

F.   "Now hold the arm to the square again while we fill the void."

Jane.   (She repeats after the facilitator.) **"In the name of Jesus Christ I petition my Heavenly Father. Please fill the void within me by giving me at this time every positive spiritual gift, intelligence, light, and anything else that I need to help me accomplish my life's mission."**

The facilitator now directs her as before to tap her chest in the middle about two inches below the collarbone while she says, "accept, (tap), accept, (tap), accept, (tap)," then hold her navel with the palm of her hand and say, "forever with me."

F.   Testing with kinesiology he asks, "Answer 'yes.' Do you now have any negative spiritual gifts?" (Test, no).
        "Answer 'yes' again. Do you have a void that needs to be filled?" (Test, no). "The void has been filled."

F.   "Even though the negative gifts that were just eliminated are very spiritual in nature, the only way they can manifest in your life is through your physical body. As they manifest physically, they produce thought patterns, habit patterns, and energy patterns that are part of your physical nature. This we could call the physical counterpart to your negative spiritual gifts. Let's measure to see just how bad that physical counterpart to your negative spiritual gifts is. We will measure it on a scale of ten. Ten is the worst it could possible be."

The facilitator tests while counting, "One (strong), two (strong), three (strong), four (strong), five (strong), six (strong), seven (weak)."

"Jane. On a scale of ten you are a seven. That is very significant. We can eliminate that by a technique called Emotional Freedom Technique, or EFT. I choose to make it as effective as possible by making it Christ centered. To do EFT, we will tap points on your body that are associated with the negative energy, thoughts, habits and emotions associated with the physical counterpart to the negative spiritual gifts. This will neutralize the negative and repatterning your body."

"We will begin by doing a little exercise called brain gym. Cross your legs at the ankle. Now extend your arms with the thumbs pointing down. Cross one hand over the other and interlock the fingers. Now rotate the arms down, around, and up, so as to have your hands and arms against your chest. Now take three deep breaths. When finished uncross the arms and legs".

"Now by closing the opposite nostril with one

finger, inhale through the right nostril, exhale through the left, inhale through the left, and then exhale through the right. The purpose of this exercise is to balance the energy in the two hemispheres of the brain."

Jane does the brain gym as instructed.

"I will now lead you through a sequence of tapping various points associated with stress and negative energy. This will not only help you release the stress and negative energy, it will reprogram your body. I will tap various points on my body to demonstrate. You are to tap each of those same points on your own body."

F.   "Hold one hand up in front of you with your palm facing toward you. Rapidly but gently tap the side of your hand between the wrist and the knuckle of the little finger. At the same time watch my finger and repeat after me."

She repeats after the facilitator while he slowly draws a circle with his finger in front of her, first one direction then the other.

Jane.   Repeating out loud after the facilitator. **"I am a child of God. Everything I am and everything I do is a reflection of him. Therefore, I choose to glorify God. I deserve a good life. I expect a good life. I claim, a good life. I create a good life. I have a good life which glorifies God and demonstrates how a child of God should live."**

F.   "Now follow my example by tapping each point seven times, rapidly and gently. Tap both sides of the body at the same time when possible. If not possible tap one side then the other."

She now imitates the facilitator as he taps the following points on his body:
    The end of each eyebrow next to the nose
    The bone at the outside corner of the eye
    The middle of the upper lip under the nose
    The middle of the lower lip
    The cheekbone directly below the center of the eye
    The collarbone near the neck
    The ribs just under the armpits
    The little fingernail
    The cheekbone again
    The collar bone again
    The sides at the base of the rib cage
    The middle fingernail
    The index fingernail
    The thumbnail
    The back of the hand between the bones that connect to the knuckles of the little finger and the ring finger. The point to be tapped is about 3/4 inch from both knuckles,

They retest, finding the stress level to be zero. They

are now ready for the nest step of the session.

Note: I find it most effective if this EFT tapping sequence is used after getting rid of all negative spiritual gifts as was done here, and then again at the end of the session.

11

TEST FOR FRAGMENTATION OF THE SPIRIT INVOLVING FRAGMENTS LARGE ENOUGH TO HAVE A PERSONALITY OF THEIR OWN. DO SOUL RETRIEVAL IF NEEDED.

When Jane was releasing the sexual abuse that came from her cousin, George, it was suspected that the abuse had caused her spirit to fragment. It is now time to deal with that possible problem.

F.   "Jane, is your spirit fragmented? In other words, are you missing any parts of your spirit?" (Test, yes).

F.   Using kinesiology to test the facilitator asks, "Jane, when you were sexually abused, did part of your spirit break away and leave because she just couldn't handle that degree of negativity?" (Test, yes).

"Are you missing any fragments that are large enough to have a personality of their own?" (Test, yes).

"Is there more than one such fragment?" (Test, yes).

"Are there more than two such fragments?" (Test, no).

F.   "Jane, imagine that you are in a beautiful meadow on a pleasant summer day. See the beautiful blue sky, the grass and wild flowers. See the trees surrounding the meadow. There are two fragments of your spirit hiding in the trees. Invite them to come out and visit with you. They will appear to be about the same age as you were when they first left. What do you see?"

Jane. "I see two little girls. One is about five, the age when my father left. The other is about eight, the age when I was sexually abused."

F.   "Tell them that the past is over and that it is time to heal. Tell them that you love them and need them, and that they need you." (There is a little pause.) "Ask them if they are willing to come back."

Jane. "They say that they are willing."

F.   "Tell them, **'I bless you with peace and love and light.'** Then, visualize a beautiful white light surrounding each of them. Invite the Savior, Jesus Christ, to come into the picture and give each one a short blessing.

As He touches each one, any residue of darkness will leave and they will become clean, pure and radiant. Let me know when the Savior has finished blessing each one."

Jane.   "He is finished."

F.   "Go to either one of these two girls. Hold both of her hands in yours. As you look into her eyes tell her, 'I love you. Welcome back.' As she looks into your eyes she will download the memory of everything she has missed out on, and as she does, she will mature very quickly and become a beautiful mature woman. Then, when you are both ready, give her a big hug. She will suddenly disappear because she has stepped inside of you, becoming part of you once again. Tell me when she is back."

Jane.   After a short pause, "She is back."

F.   "Now go to the other little girl and do the same. Tell me when she is back."

Jane.   After another short pause, "She is back."

Note: Most often when you do soul retrieval as described above, the client will be quite emotional. Sometimes the fragment will be hesitant and it will be necessary to talk to it, helping it to feel comfortable with the prospect of healing.

F.   "Jane, imagine that there is a beam of heavenly light coming down from above. It is not ordinary light. It is the Light of Christ and it can penetrate every particle of your body. Imagine that this light enters through the crown of you head and that it fills your body with light. That light will heal your spirit making sure that every part is properly bonded back together. As you visualize that light entering your body, take several deep breaths. With each breath imagine that you are inhaling light and exhaling any dark negative residue."

Jane takes several deep breaths and we are now ready to go on to the next step of the session.

12

TEST FOR FRAGMENTATION OF THE SPIRIT INVOLVING SMALL FRAGMENTS WITHOUT A PERSONALITY OF THEIR OWN. RETRIEVE THEM IF NEEDED.

F. "Many times we have little fragments of our spirit that leave for one reason or another. These little fragments are not large enough to have a personality of their own, and therefore, they will not show up when you are doing soul retrieval as we just did. These small fragments are quite different from the others. They present different problems, and they need to be dealt with in a very different manner."

"Let us now test to see if you have any such missing fragments. Jane, are you missing any such little fragments of your spirit?" (Test, yes.)

"Our spirit is composed of material that is referred to as intelligences. In other words, every part of our spirit is intelligent, and as such it can think and make decisions. There are times when we are subjected to so much stress that parts of our spirit will say, 'I can't handle this any longer. I'm out of here.' When a portion of our spirit leaves, it is not completely lost. There is a little streamer of spiritual energy that connects it back to you. This is both

60

good and bad. It is good because that spiritual connection makes it possible for that fragment to be found and retrieved. It is bad, however, because a dark entity may capture it. That little string of spiritual energy then becomes a way for that dark entity to influence you."

"Sometimes we have fragments of other people connected to us. These fragments provide a connection with that other person making it possible for him/her to negatively influence us. It is important, therefore, that we not only retrieve our missing fragments, but also rid ourselves of fragments of any another spirit that may be with us."

"We all have guardian angels who are with us to guide direct and protect. There is one thing that they will never do. They never violate our free agency. If we give them permission to help, it allows them to do much more than they otherwise could do. I suggest that we empower your guardian angels and send them out on a search and rescue mission. We can send them out to find all of your missing fragments. They can also help you rid yourself of the fragments of other spirits. Would you like to do that?"

Jane.   "Yes, I would love it."

F.   "Repeat after me."

JN.   **"I am talking to my guarding angels. I give you permission to do everything you possibly can** to help me as long as it does not interfere with the will of God. At this time I have a special mission for you. Please find every missing fragment of my spirit regardless of how long they have been gone. Even if a fragment left before birth into this life, please find everyone. If a fragment has been captured by any entity, demand its release. Achieve its release. Cleanse each fragment. Heal each fragment. Reprogram them if needed and bring them back to their perfect original state. Then integrate them back into my spirit making the spirit complete. Please find any fragments of other spirits that may be connected to me. Cleanse and heal them and take them back where they belong. Please cleanse me of any memory, negative energy, or negative residue of any kind. I accept this healing with praise, love and gratitude. I accept (tap), accept (tap), accept (tap), forever with me. (palm of hand over the navel).

A test reveals that this healing process was complete. Jane is now ready to proceed to the next step of the sequence.

13

RELEASE FEARS AND PHOBIAS AS NEEDED.

F.   "Jane, do you have any fear or phobia that you would like to eliminate at this time?"

Jane.   "Yes, I have an extreme fear of heights."

F.   "Let's measure how intense that phobia is. We will measure it on a scale of zero to ten. Ten is the very worst it could be."

At this point they test each number starting at zero and counting up. Each number results in a strong test until they get to the number eight. The number eights produces a very weak response indicating a rather intense phobia.

F.   "To release the phobia we will use the same Emotional Freedom Technique that we used before. This can be used for many different issues. The important thing is to keep in mind the issue you are releasing as you do the tapping.

"We can skip the brain gym because you did it

earlier and have already balanced the energies in the two hemispheres of the brain."

"I will now lead you through a sequence of tapping various points associated with stress and negative energy. This will help you release the stress and negative energy associated with your phobia. As before, I will tap various points on my body to demonstrate. You are to tap each of those same points on your own body."

F.   "Hold one hand up in front of you with your palm facing toward you. Rapidly but gently tap the side of your hand between the wrist and the knuckle of the little finger. At the same time watch my finger and repeat after me."

She repeats after the facilitator while he slowly draws a circle with his finger in front of her, first one direction then the other.

Jane. **"I am a child of God. Everything I am and everything I do is a reflection of him. Therefore, I choose to glorify God. I deserve a good life. I expect a good life. I claim a good life. I create a good life. I have a good life which glorifies God and demonstrates how a child of God should live."**

F.   "Now follow my example by tapping each point seven times, rapidly and gently. Tap both sides of the body at the same time when possible. If not possible tap one side then the other."

She now imitates the facilitator as he taps the following points on his body:

The end of each eyebrow next to the nose
The bone at the outside corner of the eye
The middle of the upper lip under the nose
The middle of the lower lip
The cheekbone directly below the center of the eye
The collarbone near the neck
The ribs just under the armpits
The little fingernail
The cheekbone again
The collar bone again
The sides at the base of the rib cage
The middle fingernail
The index fingernail
The thumbnail

The back of the hand between the bones that connect to the knuckles of the little finger and the ring finger. The point to be tapped is about 3/4 inch from both the little finger knuckle and the ring finger knuckle.

They retest, finding the phobia level to be zero.

Note: When I am doing this phobia cure, if the test at the end gives anything other than zero, I have the client tap four toenails all at the same time using two fingers of each hand. The toes to be tapped are the big toe of each foot and the one next to it. This time tap twenty one times. The numbers seven and twenty one are not magic. I use those numbers because they work.

Note 1: When one looks in different directions, different parts of the brain are being accessed. That is the reason why Jane is directed to watch the facilitator's finger while he draws a circle with it in front of her.

Note 2: In my first book I gave a different tapping sequence in the chapter entitled "Five Minute Phobia Cure." That one is very effective and works in most situations, but I have found that this sequence is more effective. In the past I referred to this as my "when all else fails" sequence.

14

TEST FOR RITUAL ABUSE. RELEASE AS NEEDED.

F.   "There are many people who practice witchcraft or who are involved in satanic worship, and by doing so, they have a very negative effect upon others. Some people are abused as victims of satanic ritual and have no conscious memory of that abuse. Others have curses, hexes, and spells placed upon them from a distance. In order for you and your spirit to have a clear understanding of some of the effects of ritual, I would like to give you a list of the major effects of satanic ritual and witchcraft."

Each of the following is briefly discussed. (Note: Each item listed below is a major heading in my first book in the chapter entitled "Satanic Abuse.")

1. Fragmentation of the spirit
2. Curses, hexes, and spells
3. Satanic weapons and tools
4. Shunts
5. Implants, bugs, etc.
6. Alarms
7. Triggers
8. Programs

9. Fail-safe mechanisms

10. Veils of darkness

11. Oaths, promises, and covenants

12. Negative spiritual gifts.

F.   "At this point we need to test to see if you have any of these effects of ritual."

"Do you have any effects of ritual?" (Test, yes).

F.   "Often victims of ritual are programmed on many levels. Do you have any multi-level programming?" (Test, no).

F.   "I do not perceive that you have been very deeply involved. You probably only have some hexes that were put on you from a distance. We can very quickly release them. Please raise your arm to the square and repeat after me."

Jane. **"In the name of Jesus Christ I command that all effects of satanic ritual and witchcraft be null and void. I dismiss them without argument and cancel them out, along with every spirit, thought form, energy, and residue associated with them. Cancel (tap), cancel (tap), cancel (tap), forever cancel." (She taps her thymus while saying 'cancel,' then she holds her navel while she says ' forever cancel.')**

They do a follow up test and find that there are no detectable effects of any satanic ritual or witchcraft.

Note 1: In the actual cases given in part two of this book, there will be examples of people who have been very deeply programmed. In such cases more will be required to achieve a complete release of those effects of ritual. Please refer to those examples to get the details of how to deal with the difficult cases.

Note 2: Although I have suggested that one try to follow the suggested sequence quite closely, sometime it is necessary for the sequence to be varied. For example, when doing age regression the very first thing that comes up might be ritual abuse. In such a case it would be necessary to deal with it immediately at that time.

RELEASE THE NEGATIVE PROGRAMMING FROM THE PHYSICAL SELF.

F.   "Jane, as you recall as we were releasing negative spiritual gifts, there was a physical counterpart to those physical gifts. That physical manifestation of the negative gifts was released by what is called Emotional Freedom Technique or EFT.   We also used it when dealing with a phobia. Some of the other issues that we have been releasing are also programmed into your physical nature. Using that same EFT can reprogram this negative programming. First, I would like to measure the degree of negative programming in your physical nature on a scale of zero to ten. Ten is the worst it can be."

The facilitator starts counting from zero to ten, testing each number. The arm tests weak on the number six.

F,   "Jane, in order to make the EFT effective in this new setting, all that is necessary is to keep in mind our intent. The intent here is to reprogram any remaining physical manifestation of the issues that we have been working on here today.

Because we have already used brain gym earlier to balance the energies in your brain, it will not be necessary to do it here. We can go directly into the tapping sequence.

At this point they go through the EFT tapping sequence. They then retest and find the degree of negative programming in the physical nature to be zero.

The stress level is measured again on a scale of zero to one hundred, just as was done at the beginning of the session. The stress level at this time measures three.

F   "Jane this low level of stress really means that we are finished with our session for today. In a session such as we have had here today, you and your spirit are in charge. We can only release those issues that you are ready to release. You probably have many other issues that will need to be released and given to the Lord. Those issues will have to wait for another session.

F.   "In recent years there has been a lot of research which shows a very close connection between our negative emotions and our physical problems. For example, a prominent cancer specialist said, 'I have never dealt with a cancer patient who did not have an un-forgiveness issue.'"

"Usually when one begins the healing process one can deal with only a few issues in the first session. Often there is no follow up. This leaves one with a great number of unresolved issues. I have a little book entitled 'Two Weeks to Health and Well-Being'. This book is a self-help approach to healing. It helps you continue the process that was begun today."

"Each day for fourteen days it takes you step by step through the process of finding one unresolved issue of the past and release it. Each day the issue is found in a different category including unforgiveness, guilt, addictions, distrust, and ten others."

"I strongly recommend that you take a copy of this book home with you. You will go through one short chapter each day, and will take only about ten minutes per day."

Note 1: As stated before, this generic presentation was presented, as it is here, to give a better understanding of how to proceed with each step and to put the process into a routine or algorithm that anyone can follow. Greater details will be given in many of the true examples that follow.

Note 2: It is very important that a facilitator understand how steps 6,7 and 8, of the suggest sequence interrelate. If an age regression stops you at a particular age, the next thing to do is to find the event to be released. The event will involve people and emotions. So, you are really working with all three steps at the same time. If the age regression does not trigger any memory then you start probing for events by using individuals such as father, mother, brother, sister, etc. as the trigger. When key individuals fail to bring up anything, then an emotion is used as the trigger.

No matter how the issue to be released is accessed, one cannot separate the event the people and the emotions involved. They must all be worked with together at the same time. For example, one cannot release an event without forgiving everyone involved and releasing the related emotions.

Once the emotions have been released the logical thing to do next is to get rid of the negative spiritual gifts. Most generally there will be a negative spiritual gift associated with each negative emotion.

As one facilitates the healing process, no matter how the issue to be released is accessed, there will be a natural flow as one proceeds through the steps of the suggested sequence. It will be best if one allows it to flow naturally rather than trying to force it into an exact step by step routine.

Note 3: The EFT tapping sequence is an important part of the sequence. Spiritual issues and spiritual gifts manifest through our physical bodies and create a physical counterpart to the issue or gift. If the negative physical aspect is not dealt with, often the negative spiritual aspect of the issue or negative gift will return.

There are two ideal places to use the EFT tapping sequence. The first one is immediately after releasing negative spiritual gifts. The second is at the end of the entire sequence. I like to do both. It may seem redundant but one cannot use the technique too much.

SECTION TWO

CLINICAL EXAMPLES

The following is a collection of real situations concerning real people who have been assisted by a facilitator. Names have been omitted to protect the privacy of those involved. Clients will be identified by their initials.

These examples have been selected with the intention of showing many different problems and approaches. Many of these examples will illustrate some of the previously discussed steps of spiritual healing, but in greater detail.

You will note that in each case, as much as possible, the procedure follows the clinical algorithm presented in the previous section.

1

A VERY STUBBORN SPIRIT

BJ is a woman of 47. She is married with children. She claims that for the most part, life has been good; but for several months she has had a lot of difficulty with depression and a very low level of energy.

The facilitator began in the usual way. He introduced her to kinesiology and found that he could get very clear "yes or no" type answers.

It was found that there was no problem with switching, but when checking the chakras it was found that the heart chakra was not flowing properly. This problem could very well be part of the reason for her low level of energy. The problem was corrected and they proceeded to the next step.

When he tested to see if there were any spirits present, he found that there was one devil that had been with her for several months. He began talking to it in an effort to send it to the light.

F.   "You have been controlled by Satan for millions of years. He never rewards anyone. All he ever does is punish and control by fear. I know that you hate his control but you feel trapped. Satan deceived you and has confused your mind to the point that you don't even remember who you are. You are a child of God, and Jesus Christ is your brother. They both love you and are anxious for you to return to them. All you need to do is turn to Christ and say, 'I was deceived. Please forgive me. I want to come back.' You will be accepted back with love and rejoicing. You will have your light and glory restored and you will become the glorious being you once were."

BJ.   "I can hear him speaking in my mind."

F.   "Just speak those thoughts that he puts into your mind. That way I can carry on a conversation with him."

Spirit. The spirit speaking into BJ's mind, "I won't go. I have a job to do and I must do it."

F.   "Are you saying that Satan is controlling you and you must do everything he commands?"

Spirit. "Yes, he is my master, and I must obey."

F.   "Do you enjoy being controlled by Satan?"

Spirit. "I like doing what I do, so go away and leave me alone."

F.   "You are jealous of those who have a body and are in a state of progression. You like doing what you do because it gives you a chance to vent your anger and jealousy. Isn't that true?"

Spirit. "I hate everyone, and I like to cause suffering."

F.   "Satan has told his followers that because they chose to go with him they are now subjected to eternal damnation and are therefore stuck with him forever and can do nothing about it. Satan is very good at quoting scripture and he does it often to suit his purposes, but he never quotes D. & C. 19:6-12. There the Lord explains that Eternal punishment is God's punishment, and Endless punishment is God's punishment, because Eternal and Endless are two of God's names. The scripture explains that for everyone, except those who refuse to leave Satan, Eternal punishment can come to an end. Those who stay with him will be cast out into outer darkness after the final judgment."

"You do not have to stay with him. You can be free from eternal punishment. You can go into that realm of light and love. Then there will be no reason for you to be angry or jealous."

Spirit. "I don't want to go to the light. The light will kill me."

F.   (In his mind, he blesses this spirit and commands that he be surrounded with light.) "Look at that light that surrounds you. It has not killed you. Satan lied when he told you that the light would kill you. Feel the light and you will discover that it feels good. As you feel that light you will realize that Satan has always lied to you."

Spirit. "If I try to go to the light, Christ will punish me and reject me, then Satan will punish me for trying. I cannot go to the light. I must stay here and do what I was assigned to do."

F.   "In any war, right up until the last day of battle, some warriors will wake up one morning and say, 'I have been fighting for the wrong cause.' And they defect. When they go over to the other side they are not punished. They are welcomed and invited to join with them in battle. So it is with Christ. He will welcome you with open arms. You know that Christ is a God of truth. He cannot lie. Just turn to him and ask, 'is it true? Can I be forgiven? Can I come back?' He will verify what I have said."

JB.   "I sense that he is debating what to do and is starting to look up."

F.   "You can go to the light now. Just look up. You will see your former friends waiting for you. You are free from Satan's control and abuse."

A test revealed that the spirit was gone, and that there really was nothing else that needed to be done with one exception. Sending the spirits away created a void that needed to be filled.

They went through the process of filling the void as described in part 5 of the suggested sequence. Nothing else was done at that time.

Two weeks later JB called the facilitator. She was doing fine. Her depression was gone and she had her full strength and energy back.

Note: Sending a spirit to the light is always better than just casting it out. Some of them can be very stubborn and it may take a long time and a lot of effort to convince them that they can go but it is worth it. I have spent as long as four hours talking to a spirit before it finally accepted what I was trying to teach and then accept the opportunity of going to the light.

2

NESTED SPIRITS – REJECTION

MJ is a single man age 35. He was deformed at birth. His parents have a high profile in their community and it appears as if they really do not want to be bothered with a handicapped child.

As the facilitator visited with MJ he found that he was very familiar with kinesiology testing so he did not have to introduce that concept. He found that it was very easy to get good responses to his testing.

The facilitator tested for switching and found him to be switched. This was quickly corrected.

Testing showed that all chakras were open and flowing properly.

The facilitator tested him for spirits and found that he had two. Further tasting indicated that they were both earthbound human spirits.

F.   Speaking to the two spirits: "You are in a place called spirit prison or hell. You are not here because of anything you have done. You are imprisoning yourself by your own thoughts. Because you are children of God, you have the power of creation. What you vividly visualize and think about with emotion, you create. You are focusing on many of the negative aspects of you life. By doing so, you are creating an ever repeating, never ending nightmare of the worst experiences of your life."

"You don't need to stay here in hell. Turn to Christ and ask him to take your guilt, fear, anger, or whatever you are focused on. He will replace that darkness with light. Look up. You have loved ones and friends hovering over you, waiting to take you to a better place where you can have joy. You are free to go. Please go to the light."

A test showed that one spirit was gone. The other was still there. That remaining one had to be dealt with in a very different way. It turned out that there was a problem sometimes called "nested spirits." The facilitator dealt with it as follows:

F. "MJ, I would like to talk to this spirit. I will let you answer for him with muscle testing. Just answer 'yes'."

"Am I talking to the spirit that is here with MJ?" (Test, yes).

F.   "There is darkness within you that keeps you earthbound. As you look at the darkness, does that darkness seem to have a personality of its own?" (Test, yes).

F.   "The test indicates that there is another spirit hiding inside of the one we were talking to. In other words, when the first spirit lived upon the earth as a mortal, there was a spirit hiding inside of him, just as this spirit is now hiding inside of you, MJ. When that person died, the spirit stayed inside, where he had been. Thus there is a spirit possessing another spirit. The two of them are now here with you."

"I would like to talk to the second spirit. I will call him number two."

"Number two, as you look at the darkness within yourself, does it seem to have a personality of it's own?" (Test, yes).

F.   "There is a third spirit hiding inside of number two. I will call it number three. Number three, as you look at the darkness within yourself, does that darkness seem to have a personality of its own?" (Test, yes).

F.   "There is a fourth spirit inside of number three. Number four, does the darkness within yourself seem to have a personality of its own?" (Test, no).

This time the test indicated that this is the inner most spirit. Further testing revealed that this one was a devil. The facilitator continues by talking to that devil.

F.   "I know what you are doing. You are hiding from

Satan. He has never rewarded you for anything. All he ever does is punish and control by fear, and you hate it. Isn't that true?" (Test, yes).

F.　　"The time has come for you to become free from Satan's control and abuse. Satan deceived you, and he has confused your mind to the point that you don't even remember who you are. You are a child of God and Jesus Christ is your brother. They both love you and are anxious for you to return to them."

"All you need to do is to call out to Christ and say, 'I was deceived. Please forgive me. I want to be with you.' He will take all the darkness from you and replace it with light. You will become the glorious being that you once were. You are now free to go the light. As you look up you will see former loved ones and friends waiting for you. Please go with them."

"Now I am talking to number three again. Number three, did that spirit number four go to the light? (Test, yes).

F.　　"Number three, now that the dark spirit has gone, you are free to give your burdens to Christ. Give him your negative thoughts, feelings and emotions. He will cleanse you. Look up. There are loved ones waiting to take you to a better place. Go with them to the light."

"Number two, you can do the same."

"Number one, now you can also do the same. Go

to the light."

Testing revealed that all the spirits were gone.

F.   "MJ, it is possible for a spirit to enter at the time of birth. When that happens we tend to accept that spirit as becoming part of us, just as the body has now become part of us. Instead of recognizing that spirit as a foreign entity, we see it as a big bundle of spiritual gifts and we bond to it. For that reason the tests we have been using to find the dark spirits often do not work. Now that you and your spirit understand that concept, I would like your spirit to look for any such spirits. Are there any such spirits with you? Hold." (Test, yes). Further testing revealed three.

F.   "MJ, these spirits usually are not real dark evil spirits. These are well meaning spirits that are trying to live their life again through you, but it doesn't work. They probably think that they are contributing something positive to your life. They have darkness that keeps them earth bound and that darkness has a negative effect upon you. It is time for them to go to the light. Please talk to those spirits by repeating after me."

MJ.   Repeating after the facilitator, **"Now that I know you are there, and that you are not a part of me, I apologize for bonding to you and clinging to you. I release you. You are now free to go to the light just as the others did."**

A test reveals that all of them were gone.

F.   "Those spirits have been with you for so long they have become part of your comfort zone. It is important that we fill the void that has been created. If we do not, you will feel as if you have lost some of your best friends. To fill that void, please repeat after me."

MJ.   MJ repeats after the facilitator. **"In the name of Jesus Christ I petition my Heavenly Father. Please fill the void within me by giving me at this time every positive spiritual gift, light, intelligence, and anything else I need to help me fulfill my life's mission. Accept, accept, accept, forever with me." He taps his thymus as he says 'accept', and holds his navel as he says 'forever with me.'**

The facilitator next measured MJ's stress level and found it to be in the low 70s. When he did an age regression nothing came up, so he started looking for stress that was more connected to family members than to some time frame. They quickly found that both father and mother were big sources of stress.

As they visited about his parents, he revealed that his parents had not given him the love and attention he needed. They were high profile in the community and they acted as if they were embarrassed to claim him. They gave him only the minimum required care and he spent most of his time alone in his bedroom.

For the last four or five years MJ has been living with someone who has been hired to care for him. He has been living in another state away from home, and his parents would not invite him to move back home. Needless to say, he felt very rejected. Before proceeding they tested several other emotions. There was a weak response when testing hate, fear, rejection, anger, low self-esteem, and resentment. These negative emotions all seemed to be connected to his parents.

F.   "MJ, please cup your hand and with it hold your forehead gently. This will give you biofeedback that will help you deal with stress. Get a picture of your father in your mind's eye. Now talk to your father in your own words. Tell him that you love him. Tell him that the past is over and that it doesn't matter any more except for what the two of you can learn. Forgive your father for anything he ever said or did or that he didn't say or didn't do that offended you. Ask him to forgive you for anything that offended him. Then tell him once again that you love him. Let me know when you are finished."

There was a pause while he processed, and then he gave a little nod.

F.   "Now I would like you to repeat what you just did

with one little addition. Visualize a beam of white light connecting your heart to your father's heart while you express love and forgiveness as before."

There is another pause while he processed, then he gave a little nod.

F.   "By visualizing that beam of white light connecting your heart to your father's heart, you are creating a positive bond with your father. Please go through that process one more time."

F.   "Now get a picture of your mother in your mind's eye and just as you did with your father, tell her that you love her. Tell her that the past is over and that it doesn't matter any more except for what the two of you can learn. Forgive your mother for anything she ever said or did or that she did not say or did not do that offended you. Ask her to forgive you for anything that offended her. Then tell her once again that you love her. Let me know when you are finished."

Just as he did with his father, he went through this visualization then repeated it while visualizing a beam of white light connecting his heart to his mother's heart.

F.   "MJ, think of your mother and father."   (The facilitator tested and got a very strong positive response.)

F.   "Do you believe that people can receive special gifts from the Holy Spirit?"

MJ.   "Yes."

F.   "There is opposition in all things. This concept guarantees that just as the Holy Spirit can give you a gift, so can Satan. When the Holy Spirit gives you a gift, it increases your ability to perform in a positive way. When Satan gives you a spiritual gift, it increases your ability to perform in a negative way. Let us now check to see if you have any negative spiritual gifts. To do this, I will name many of the possible negative spiritual gifts. I will test the arm after naming each gift. If there is no problem your arm will remain locked. If Satan has succeed in giving you that gift, the arm will become weak."

They tested and found the following negative gifts: hate, fear, rejection, anger, low self-esteem, and resentment.

F.   "MJ, when you raise your arm to the square it acts as an antenna to draw spiritual energy into you and by doing so you magnify and increase the power of the spoken words. To release these negative gifts I need you to raise your arm to the square and repeat after me.

MJ.   He repeats after the facilitator. **"In the name of Jesus Christ I command that all negative spiritual gifts depart. I dismiss them without argument and cancel them out, along with every spirit, thought form, energy, and residue associated with them. Cancel, cancel, cancel. Forever cancel."**

While saying, "cancel," he taps the chest over the thymus. While saying, "Forever cancel" he holds his navel with the palm of one hand.

F. "Now hold the arm to the square again while we fill the void."

MJ,   (He repeats after the facilitator.) **"In the name of Jesus Christ I petition my Heavenly Father. Please fill the void within me by giving me at this time every positive spiritual gift, intelligence, light, and anything else that I need to help me accomplish my life's mission."**

A follow-up test indicates that all the negative spiritual gifts had been eliminated.

F. "We have released the negative gifts from your spirit, but you have negative programming in you physical nature that is the physical counterpart to those negative spiritual gifts. This programming should be eliminated also. Let's check to see how bad that negative programming is on a scale of zero to ten."

At this point the facilitator counts up zero, one, two three, etc. testing after each number. The arm is locked on every number until the number nine. The number nine resulted in a weak test indicating a very high degree of negative programming. To eliminate that negative programming the facilitator guided him through "brain gym" followed by the EFT tapping sequence. (This is given for your convenience in the appendage at the back of the book).

A follow up test showed the programming level to be zero. Other follow up tests showed the stress level to be at three, and that there was nothing else that we could do at that time.

Note: Always there are other problems, but one cannot do too much at one time or it becomes counter productive. I suspect that on a follow up session it will be found that his spirit is fragmented and he may have some phobias. The facilitator tried to address those issues in this session but MJ was not ready to proceed with that part of the normal sequence.

3

BABY SITTER

The following session was the facilitator's first session with a 57-year-old woman whom I will refer to by her initials AG. The facilitator asked her what she wanted to accomplish in her session with him. She responded that she seemed to be doing a lot of self-defeating things. For example, she often did little unimportant chores as a way of avoiding doing the more important things.

Because this type of behavior could be the result of negative programming that could have come from many different sources, it was suggested that they proceed, allowing her spirit to bring out anything that the spirit was ready to process.

AG had heard of kinesiology muscle testing but had no previous experience with it. It was introduced to her by going through the procedure as given in this books introductory chapter.

She was quite surprised at how the testing worked but she responded very quickly and was very easy to test.

When tested for being switched it was found that

she was switched and that was quickly corrected.

The chakras were tested and it was found that all chakras were open and flowing properly.

The facilitator told her that he would like to test some of her energy fields. Without really telling her what he was doing, he tested for negative entities and found three present. When he explained to her how spirits could be present, AG accepted the explanation, so he continued by explaining that the test he had just done with her indicated that she had three spirits attached to her. Her response was that she had suspected for quite some time that she had such a problem. She was anxious to rid herself of those visitors.

He asks with kinesiology, "Are any of the spirits present the kind we refer to as devils?" AG answered, "yes." He then tested and got a weak test which indicated that the answer was "no." He knew that the spirits that were present were the kind known as unclean, so he spoke directly to them explaining where they were and why.

He explained that they were in a state of stagnation in a realm known as spirit prison. They are not imprisoned because of what they did during their life on earth as mortals. Instead, they are imprisoned by their thoughts, feelings, and emotions. When they passed through the change we call death, they focused their thoughts, feelings, and emotions on the negative aspects of their life. By doing so, they created the dark negative energy that has kept them earthbound. He told them that they were literally trapping themselves in an ever repeating, never-ending nightmare of the worst experiences of their life.

He continued by inviting each of these spirits to give their burdens to Christ and promised them that by doing so Christ would heal them replacing the darkness with light and love. The spirits left rather easily.

They checked to see if any spirits had come at the time of birth. The test indicated that none were present.

He then asked, with a test, if dismissing the spirits had created a void that needed to be filled. The answer was yes. They filled the void by having AG raise her arm to the square and repeat the following:

AG.   She repeated after the facilitator. **"In the name of Jesus Christ, the only begotten son of the Father, I petition my Heavenly Father; please fill the void within me by giving me at this time every positive spiritual gift, light, intelligence, and shield of protection that I am ready to receive and capable of using at this time to help me fulfill my life's mission."**

Note: I usually consider everything that has transpired up to this point to be preliminary. It is all very important and they could not proceed without taking care of these problems.   I consider this work preliminary because, although the presence of spirits is a major contributing factor, they had not directly addressed any of

the issues that caused AG to come to for help. At this point
they were finally ready to look for the source of her stress
and to help her release it.

F.   "Every experience of life leaves a residue of energy.
It can be either positive or negative. The negative will stay
with us until it is released. This accumulation of negative
energy is the source of the stress with which we are dealing.
If something can be measured, then one can tell if progress
is being made. For that reason I like to measure the stress.
I do this on a scale of zero to one hundred. Using
kinesiology we can measure that stress."

They measured her stress and found it to be 83.

The next step was to do an age regression, which
indicated that something happened at age three.

F.   "AG, do you have any memory of something
negative happening at the age of three?"

AG.   "No. I have no memories that go back that far."

F.   "Well, let's see what we can find. I would like to
test some key words. Think of Father, (Test strong). Think
of Mother, (Test Strong).   Brothers, Sisters and extended
family also resulted in a strong test.
        "AG, let's see if we can locate the source of this

stress by relating it to some emotion.   Think of fear, hold."
(Test, strong). "Think of rejection, hold."   (Test, strong).
"Abuse, hold." (Test, weak). "AG, it seems as if there was
some kind of abuse. Think of father, hold." (Test, strong).
"Mother, hold." (Test, strong).

They continued the probing by testing brothers,
sisters, grandparents, neighbors, etc.   Finally he asked,
"Think of baby sitter, hold." (Test, very weak).

They didn't know who the baby sitter was, nor did
they know the nature of the abuse. Asking questions with
kinesiology it seemed apparent that AG had been crying
after the parents left her with the baby sitter. Instead of
trying to comfort this little three-year-old girl, the baby
sitter used some form of harsh punishment, even to the
point of traumatizing this little child. It is truly amazing
how such experiences can affect one throughout one's
entire life until the experience is processed and released.

AG visualized going into a beautiful meadow where
she invited the baby sitter to come and visit with her. The
facilitator walked AG through the process of visualizing the
baby sitter and talking to her as follows:

AG.   **"The past is over. It really does not matter
any more except for what we can learn from it. I
forgive you and release you. I will not judge you
because I do not understand your background,**

and the things that led you to the point where you would treat me the way you did. I will only love you."

At this point AG took several deep breaths. As she inhaled she imagined that she was inhaling light. As she exhaled, she imagined that she was exhaling and releasing all the dark negative energy associated with the baby sitter.

AG then imagined that she had a time machine and could go back in time and visit that sad frightened little three-year-old girl. In her mind, she held her, comforted her, and loved her. She told the little girl that it was all over and didn't matter any more except for what she could learn.

The facilitator explained the concept of negative spiritual gifts then tested to see if AG had any negative spiritual gifts. Testing revealed two. They were low self-esteem and doubt. These were sent away and canceled out and the void was filled as described in Section One.

Although this was not yet verified by kinesiology, the facilitator had a very strong feeling that the trauma had caused a fragmentation of the spirit. He proceeded, acting on that assumption. A test revealed that in fact there was a three-year-old fragment that was missing.

He walked AG through the process of visualizing herself in a very peaceful meadow. The three-year-old was invited into the meadow. AG was walked through the process of blessing the little three-year-old with light and love, then inviting the Savior into the picture. Christ blessed the little girl drawing from her all the darkness, fear, and pain. AG then held the little one in her arms and she quickly stepped inside and became part of the adult AG.

A test showed that most, but not all, the stress was gone.

At this point they tested to see if there were any minor fragments of the spirit not big enough to have a personality of their own. The test showed that there was one. This one was retrieved by sending AG's guardian angels on a search and rescue mission as described on page 60.

When the facilitator asked what else was causing stress, she indicated that her daughter was not living right and that it was causing a lot of stress.

It has been found from experience that when children are properly bonded to their parents there is much less chance that the child will act out in negative ways, so it was suspected that AG was not properly bonded to her daughter.

F.   The facilitator tested while asking, "Do you have a good strong positive bond with your daughter?" They got a weak response indicating that the answer was "no."

AG was guided through another visualization session. This time she visualized her daughter. She then visualized the Light of Christ filling her own body, concentrating near her heart. This light, the light of love, was then sent from AG's heart to her daughter forming a positive bond. This was visualized as a string of light permanently connecting heart to heart. AG reported seeing dark strings connecting her to her daughter. These were bonds of control. AG cut each negative bond while telling the daughter, "I release you. We will not try to control each other any more."

F.   "AG, imagine yourself in a very peaceful place with your daughter. Visualize a bright string of light connecting you to your daughter, heart to heart. I will help you send a message of love and forgiveness over that positive bond.

AG.   Repeating after him, **"I love you. I forgive you for everything you ever said or did or didn't say or didn't do that offended me. Please forgive me for the things that offended you. I love you."**

AG repeated this visualization two more times. A follow up test showed the level of stress related to her daughter was at the zero level.

AG was asked if she had any phobias that bothered her. She said there were none so they proceeded to the next step in the sequence.

F.   "AG, there are many people who practice various forms of witchcraft. They try to influence and control others through the use of their witchcraft. Do you have any such negative influences affecting you in any way? (Test, no).

The facilitator explained that what they had done to this point was primarily directed to the healing of the spirit. These same issues can also affect the physical body with "negative programming." He then asked her spirit to measure the degree of negative programming in the physical body. This was measured on a scale of zero to ten using kinesiology. The test showed that the degree of negative programming was a six. She released this by using brain gym and the EFT tapping sequence as given in the appendage at the back of the book. A follow up test showed the negative programming in the physical nature to be zero.

Getting zero on a stress test, and zero on the test for negative programming does not mean that all issues have been released. What it means is that they have processed everything that could be dealt with at that time. The session was finished.

4

WALK-INS

As we work with people, trying to help them heal the inner self, we are dealing primarily with the realm of spirit. Because our three dimensional realm of mortality is so different from the dimension of the spirit, sometimes it becomes very difficult to understand what seems to be going on in that other realm. Sometimes it even seems so strange that we cannot believe what seems to be happening.

I have found that if I do not ask, "Is this really true?" and just go forward, great steps can be made in the healing process. As a result, I have found that it does not matter whether or not the concepts with which we are dealing are absolutely true. The client's perception is what really matters. It is that perception which has affected the client. I therefore, just accept situations at face value and proceed. This open-minded approach has led me into some really strange situations, but those strange situations invariably result in dynamic improvement. The following is one such case.

This case involves a woman whom I will refer to only by initials CC.

This is a woman in her late 70's. She has had several sessions before and although the prior sessions were productive, when she came before she was not ready to deal with what might be called the real heavy stuff.

The facilitator made sure that he could get good answers using kinesiology. They checked and found that there was no problem with being switched, and the chakras were all open and flowing properly.

Before the facilitator could test for spirit attachments, she pulled out a notebook and asked if she could read what she had written. The following came from that notebook:

CC.   "I woke up this morning crying. I was crying for my children, and for my lack of ability, while they were growing up, to protect them, to help them feel secure, to strengthen them for what life had already dealt them, what they were dealing with presently, and to bravely meet what was ahead for them."

"I cried too, for me: for what I had dealt with in my life that diminished my ability to become what I wanted to be for my children."

"Many horrible life experiences have been hidden so deep inside of my psyche that only constant study, counseling, praying, and healing therapy has helped bring them to the surface, only to be kept hidden in the secret chambers of my heart to protect those I love. I'm thinking that the reason some of these unpleasant happenings surfaced this morning was to let me know it was time to let it all come out, and to quit covering for my ex-husband, and especially for Dad."

"Maybe most of the trauma stemmed from my early interactions with my father. I have already told about being sexually molested by my uncle. It went on most of one summer. Are any of you aware of the damage that does to a child? Read about it and find out. It's not pretty."

"When Dad found out, he told his brother to get out of the house and get going. I can imagine his rage as he did so. But, Dad also said to me, 'I'll kill him! I'll kill him! I'll kill him!' I remember nothing else being said to me. I didn't even know if my mother knew what had happened. She didn't say anything to me -- ever."

"I lived the rest of my life with a horrible burning guilt. I felt totally unworthy of anything. I was not good enough for anything or anybody. I felt that it was my fault if anything bad happened to anyone close to me."

"When the uncle who abused me died, Dad started out for his funeral, but he had a wreck along the way. Of course I felt it was my fault. I was sure Dad wrecked on purpose because he really didn't want to go to the funeral. I was sure it was my fault because I had spoiled their relationship."

"Let me tell you about the beating Dad gave me with a board because I went wading with a neighbor boy after Dad told me not to wade in the ditch."

"Can you imagine how it hurt to be beaten with a board? He beat me on my bottom until I covered it with my hands, then on my legs and on and on. I didn't know why, but I felt that the beating was because he didn't trust me with a boy. I can't remember what he said, but he was saying some awful things. I remember that much. Mostly, I think I wondered how my Dad, whom I loved, could be so cruel."

"I believe that the words he said and the way he said them damaged me even more than the molesting by my uncle. Can you imagine what I felt when Dad said, 'I'll kill him?' I cry now as I write it. At least my uncle was kind to me otherwise."

"Those experiences were bad enough but I do remember them. This next one was so devastating that most of it was taken from my memory. I'm sure that accounts for the vagueness and the unrealness that I have always felt in regards to my life."

CC then went on to tell how she one day went to her father's place of work and walked into his office without knocking. She caught him in the act of having sex with a woman. Of course the woman fled and he dressed himself. He then grabbed her by the neck and while squeezing threatened to kill her if she ever told what she had seen.

CC had previously come for help and had released much of the stress and dark negative energy of the past, but these issues had not come up. Much had been dealt with but these heavy details had not come forth. (I have found that in a session the only things that will come forth are the things one is ready to process and release.) In CC's case many of the real heavy issues had remained buried until now. As a result she was still struggling.

Along with other things, she felt strongly that she had some serious sex hang ups that made it very difficult for her to have a healthy intimate sexual relationship in marriage. Her perception was that even though her uncle had molested her regularly all one summer, that had not damaged her as much as her father's reaction to the situation. When her father exclaimed in great anger, "I'll kill him!" it programmed her subconscious with a belief that if she had a sexual relationship with anyone, even her husband, her father would kill him.

As the facilitator listened to CC pour her heart out, he asked himself, how do you release such a problem? Several options came to mind.

As always, he began by testing to see if there were any negative entities present with her. He did this with kinesiology. First, testing with the arm while holding the back of the neck. With this test, a weak response would have indicated the presence of a spirit. The results were mushy and inconclusive. He next tested the arm while holding her forehead gently with the palm of his other hand. In this test a strong response would have indicated the presence of a spirit. Again the response was mushy and inconclusive. Both tests led him to believe that there was a hidden entity present. He told CC that he felt that there were some unwanted spirits present.

She responded by expressing her perception. She believed that as a child, because of the negative experiences with her father, her spirit, the center core that is the eternal part of her, was so fearful and wounded that she wanted to die. She believed that the major portion of her spirit had in fact departed from her body and that a positive spirit assigned to help her fulfill her earthly mission immediately took possession of her body. She felt that this occurred to keep the body alive until her spirit could heal to the point that she could return and resume her rightful place in the body and take full responsibility. CC referred to this spirit who had taken possession of her body as a "walk-in."

CC further explained her belief that from time to time her spirit returned to "be taught" but she never healed to the point that she could resume her position and responsibility within the body. Thus, CC believed that she had been under the influence of a "walk-in" almost all of her life

As stated before, in such a situation I do not question a person's belief system. The issue is not whether or not her perception is true or false. It is her perception that creates the problems. The important thing is to deal with the problem and help her heal. The facilitator proceeded with the assumption that her perception was accurate.

If CC's perception were really true, her spirit

needed to heal and come back before the "walk-in" could be dismissed. Therefore, instead of immediately trying to dismiss the "walk-in" the facilitator decided to first work with the trauma that initiated the problem in the first place. He felt that once the problem was resolved, the "walk-in" problem could more easily be dealt with.

The facilitator proceeded by walking her through a short meditation. He did this while gently holding her forehead with the palm of one hand and at the same time stabilizing her head by placing the other hand at the lower part of the back of her head. The reason for holding the head in this manner is that it gives the body biofeedback, which causes the body to produce a small quantity of endorphin. This positive body chemistry helps one deal with stress. That is why nature's way of dealing with stress is to gently hold your forehead with the palm of the hand.

F.   "CC, where is your favorite place to relax and feel perfectly safe and at ease?"

CC.   "I like the mountains."

F.   "Imagine you are in a beautiful meadow with beautiful blue sky, a pleasant summer breeze, lots of green grass, and lots of wild flowers. Let it be a place of peace and beauty. Can you see it? Are you there?"

CC.   "Yes, I can see it clearly."

F.   "Now invite your father to come into the meadow with you."

Once she got an image of her father in mind, she was guided through the process of forgiving him and letting go of the past. She told him that she would not judge him, but rather she loved him and accepted him. She then told him that she forgave him for everything that had offended her, and especially those things that created within her the emotions and thoughts of fear and guilt. She then asked him to forgive her for anything that had offended him. She again expressed her love for him. She then repeated this entire visualization again.

A kinesiology test indicated that her stress over her father was gone, but she still was struggling with the emotions of guilt, fear, and rejection.

They approached those negative emotions by treating them as negative spiritual gifts. A test revealed that if fact, she did have negative spiritual gifts of guilt, fear and rejection. She was instructed to raise her arm to the square and repeat the following:

CC.   **"In the name of Jesus Christ, the only begotten son of the Father, I command all negative spiritual gifts to depart. Especially I command the gifts of guilt, fear, and rejection to depart. I dismiss them without argument and cancel them out along with every spirit, thought-form, energy,**

program, and residue associated with them. Cancel. Cancel. Cancel. Forever cancel."

As she said cancel she tapped the middle of her chest above the thymus gland. This is located about two inches below the collarbone. Doing this stimulates the spiritual thymus helping the spirit to heal. While saying, "forever cancel" she held her hand over the navel to draw spiritual energy in through the navel to strengthen the spirit.

Note: She did not feel comfortable with the idea of raising her arm to the square. So, I first explained why I had her do it. The ancient Chinese studied spiritual energy. They called it Chi. They found that when you raise your arm to the square it acts as an antenna to draw spiritual energy into you, and by doing so it magnifies the power of the spoken words.

A kinesiology test revealed that those negative gifts were completely gone. The void was filled as described in section 10 of the suggested sequence.

The facilitator explained that releasing the negative spiritual gifts was a process for healing the spirit. But there is a physical counterpart to those spiritual gifts. The physical body is usually programmed with patterns that are similar to those that affect the spirit and often have to be dealt with separately. Sometimes the physical nature will heal along with the spiritual. On other occasions, the physical needs special attention.

To determine if her physical nature needed special help, the facilitator asked, using kinesiology, "On a scale of zero to ten, how badly are you programmed with the physical counterpart to those negative spiritual gifts?" The test showed a level of zero. This meant that they could skip this phase of the session. Had he gotten any level above zero he would have used the EFT tapping sequence to release the programming from the physical nature.

They were now ready to deal with the "walk-ins." He started talking directly to the "walk-in." He did this by asking CC to allow the spirit to speak into her mind and for her to respond by verbalizing any thought that came into her mind, not questioning the source of the thought.

Both CC and the facilitator were surprised by what came out. They did get a spirit to respond, but it was not the "walk-in." The spirit that responded claimed to be CC's son who died at the time of his birth. All indications were that he had attached himself to his mother at the time of birth and had been with her ever since.

He really did not know what his options were. He did not understand why he was trapped in the lower realm of the spirit world nor did he know where else he could go or how to get there. He therefore needed to be taught some basic truths concerning the spirit world. The discussion was as follows:

F.   "There is a book that was first published about 1951 or 1952, entitled 'Life In The World Unseen' by Anthony Borgia. This book tells of a Reverend Benson who had some wonderful spiritual gifts and had seen spirits many times. He had written books in which he talked about seeing spirits and explained it according to his church's accepted doctrine."

"When he died and passed on into the world of spirit, he found that most of what he had written was incorrect. He kept begging the Lord to let him come back to earth and appear to someone. He wanted to set the record straight. After a few years he was given that permission."

"He appeared to his nephew, Anthony Borgia, who wrote the words as dictated to him by the dead uncle. The book is written in the first person as if the dead uncle himself is speaking from the spirit world. He gives the most accurate and interesting description of the spirit world I have ever heard."

"The Reverend describes the spirit world as consisting of seven planes parallel to the surface of the earth, each plane being better than the one below it. The upper five planes are levels of light and are collectively known as paradise. The two lower planes are levels of darkness. The lowest of these seven planes coincides with the surface of the earth. That lowest plane is the darkest one. It is the place referred to in scripture as hell. It is also known as spirit prison."

"There are at least two different classes of spirits who dwell in the lower dark plane. Those rebellious spirits who have never had a body, that we refer to as devils, are there. Along with the devils are a great many earthbound spirits of people who have lived and died. This latter group of spirits are often referred to as unclean spirits. They are called unclean because of the dark, negative energy that keeps them earthbound."

"Because that lowest spirit plane is right here on the surface of the earth, both the devils and the unclean spirits see us and influence us in many ways. These are the spirits that often enter our bodies or our energy fields, bringing their negative energy with them. These are the ones spoken of in scripture wherein you read of Christ casting out unclean spirits."

"Although we speak of the unclean spirits being in spirit prison, it is important that we understand that they are not imprisoned because of their sins. They are imprisoned by their thoughts, feelings, and emotions. When they passed through death they focused their thoughts, feelings, and emotions on the negative aspects of life such as guilt, shame, hate, rejection, revenge etc. Those thoughts and emotions create negative energy that kept them earthbound. Christ said, 'Cast your burdens upon me.' When these spirits turn to Christ, asking him to take all their negative thoughts, feelings, and emotions, He will take them all, replacing the darkness with light and love. That is called making the atonement of Jesus Christ work. When those spirits look up they will see angels of light waiting to take them up into that realm of light and love known as Paradise."

All of this was explained to CC's son and CC tried to dismiss him and send him on his way to a better place. He still would not leave. He insisted that he loved his mother and did not want to leave her.

Again they had to return to the teaching mode. The Facilitator explained to him that even though he was well intentioned, the fact was, he was earth bound. That alone is an indication that he carried with him a great deal of negative energy. He in turn was bringing that negative energy into his mother causing harm. If such a spirit really wants to help someone, he should first go to the light and become healed; then should he return, he would return as an angel of light able to truly help instead of hinder.

The spirit left and CC felt a great relief.

Again they tried to talk to the "walk-in" by letting him speak into CC's mind. This time they were able to make contact. This spirit claimed to be neither a devil nor an unclean spirit. He claimed to be a spirit from the realm of light sent to take charge of CC's body until her spirit was ready to take over again.

My experience indicates that what I call your "center core" can leave, but a small portion of your spirit must stay behind. Otherwise the body would die. It was this major portion of CC's spirit that they were trying to retrieve.

F.   "CC, imagine yourself in a beautiful meadow. Now invite that missing part of you to join you there.

CC saw her, in her minds eye, as a beautiful younger version of herself.

It was explained to this portion of CC's spirit that the past was over and it did not matter except for what could be learned from it, and that the problems of the past were now nothing but an illusion. There was no need or reason for fear, hate, guilt or any other problem of the past. CC's spirit agreed to resume her proper position within the body and to accept the responsibility that goes with it. CC visualized bright light surrounding this spirit. Then it entered her. Immediately thereafter, testing showed that the "walk-in" was gone. Apparently it was no longer needed.

CC said that although she had never had any problem with same sex attraction, she always felt quite masculine. As she was growing up, she was a tomboy and seldom played with girl toys or wore feminine clothes. Both the son and the "walk-in" were male spirits. This would explain her masculine tendencies. After both of those spirits left, she immediately felt much more feminine.

As I said before, keeping an open mind and accepting everything at face value will lead one into some interesting and strange new concepts. I have heard people talk about the concept of "walk-ins" before, but this was the first session I have known about where this concept came into the session. This session with CC also had another interesting twist.

CC told about her father being a twin. His twin sister was born deformed and died at birth.

At one time, recently, CC had a very vivid dream in which she saw a woman delivering twins, a boy and a girl. The girl was very deformed. Because of her condition the medical staff made no effort to save her life. This little one was dumped into a garbage bag where she smothered and died very quickly.

CC believes that she was the little deformed baby, and that she was given another chance to gain a body. She has always had a fear of being smothered. She believed that this dream explained the origin of that phobia.

She believes that her father was really her brother in that very short prior life. In that life, he hated her and "kicked her out." Before birth he robbed her of proper nutrition causing her to be badly deformed. She also believed that the same animosity carried over into this life. Whether this is true or not does not really matter. The point is, as long as she believed it, those beliefs had a profound affect upon the way she viewed her father.

Again they proceeded on the assumption that what

CC believed was true.

F.   "CC, imagine that you have a time machine and that you can go back to the time you were born as a very undernourished deformed little baby. Forgive your twin and tell him that the past is over and that it doesn't matter any more. Tell him that you love him and that you release him. Tell the little baby girl that the past is over and that it is time to let go of the past and move on."

There was a pause while CC processed that issue, and then they tested and found the stress associated with that issue of a "past life" was gone.

CC went through the process of releasing the phobia of being smothered by first doing the brain gym exercise then the EFT tapping sequence. The phobia was completely gone.

After dealing with all perceived issues relating to her father, for the first time in many years, CC could think about her father without having any negative thoughts, feelings, or emotions.

Both CC and the facilitator felt that this session was a great success.

Note 1: There are many ways in which one can have a memory of a past life that is really a life that was lived by another person. In other words, one can borrow the memory of someone else's life. Such a memory can affect you as much as if you lived that life yourself. For that reason, whether you believe in reincarnation or not, I have found that past life therapy can be very effective.

Note 2: This session illustrates the fact that although the facilitator tries to follow the suggested sequence, the client and the client's spirit are in charge of the session and they often lead you through the session in the way that is best for them.

5

SURROGATE HELP

GW is a married woman of about 28 years of age. She has had some problems with allergies, but nothing life threatening. She went out with her family to a restaurant for dinner and a pleasant night out. The indications were that there were some chemicals in the food that she was eating, which triggered the worst episode of allergic reaction she had ever experienced.

She was rushed to the hospital emergency facility for treatment. Her vital organs such as liver, kidney and spleen shut down and she had to be admitted into intensive care. Her prognosis was very grim.

Her sister in-law called me and told me of her condition. She wanted to know if there was anything that I could do for her.

Using my wife as a surrogate, I tested and found that she had several very dark spirits with her. Spirits communicate by thought transfer and distance does not make any difference, so I began talking to those spirits in my mind. I explained to them where they were and why. I told them that they were in a realm called Spirit Prison or

Hell. I also explained, "You are not in prison because of anything you have done. You are there because of your thoughts, feelings and emotions. If you will just turn to Christ and ask, He will take that negativity from you and replace it with the thoughts and energy of light and love.

I said to them, "Look up. You will see loved ones and friends hovering over you, anxious to take you to a better place where they can live with you in love and peace." I then said, "You are free. Please let go of the issues of the past and go to the light."

The kinesiology test indicated that they were gone.

I did not think much more about it until a day or two later. GW's sister in-law called to report on her condition. She said that immediately after she called me, GW started to improve. The very next day she walked out of the intensive care unit, was released from the hospital and went home. The doctor said that in all of his years of medical practice he had never known of anyone ever walking out of the intensive care unit.

All the patients, whom he had known in the past, were so sick and weak that when they left the intensive care unit they were wheeled out. From the intensive care unit they always went to another area of the hospital to continue their recovery prior to being released to go home.

6

SATANIC RITUAL

AK is a married woman of 37. She has been married three times but at this time she is single again. She has two children but both of them are in the custody of their father. She has been dealing with a great deal of depression and recently she has manifested an obsessive-compulsive behavior disorder. She keeps washing her hands. She had washed her hands so much they were becoming raw and chapped.

AK was familiar with kinesiology muscle testing, and the facilitator was able to get very clear discernable answers from the testing.

He tested and found that she was switched. This problem was quickly corrected.

Her heart chakras was not and flowing correctly. This was quickly corrected.

When testing for spirit attachments it was found that she had three, one devil and two unclean. They were sent to the light and they all left quickly.

There were no spirits that came at the time of birth.

The facilitator tested her stress level and found it to be ninety-three on a scale of zero to one hundred. That is extremely high. Usually those who test above 90 have had some problems with suicidal tendencies.

He next did an age regression which took her immediately back to the time of birth.

F.   "Do you know anything concerning your birth?"

AK.   "No, not really. I do know that I came late and was rather large. Other than that, I think the pregnancy and my delivery were quite normal."

An overdue delivery is often an indication that there is a fear of failure and a fear of the problems associated with mortality, or even a desire to avoid birth. It is possible that many stillbirths are the result of the spirit of the unborn baby opting not to accept mortality.

F.   "AK, Imagine that you have a time machine and you can go back to the time of birth. Think of fear of failure." (Test, weak). "Now think of the fear of life in general." (Again the test was very weak).

"AK, I believe that every one of us had an interview with God, our Heavenly Father, before we were born. We were given an opportunity to choose what we wanted to accomplish on earth. You might say we made up our shopping list, and Heavenly Father made up a list of trials and challenges. For everything on our list, Heavenly Father listed a series of trials and challenges that we needed to help us achieve the growth we were seeking. Because time is different there, He could take us into the future. He showed us exactly what our life would be like with all those challenges. We were looking at life from a celestial perspective. We accepted each challenge thinking that we could easily handle everyone of them."

"We came down from that celestial realm at the time of conception and we were able to see the problems of mortality from quite a different perspective. We could tune into the thoughts, feelings and emotions of every one around us. We could see and hear everything that was going on around us, and truly we became aware that this world could be a real challenge. As a result, many of us had second thoughts when it was time to be born."

"AK, apparently you were one who, at the point of birth, became very fearful of life on earth. Let's ask your spirit if that is true. (Test, yes). We need to release that fear."

"When one's forehead is held gently the body has biofeedback which creates some very positive body chemistry. This helps one deal with stress. Have you ever noticed how people hold their forehead when under stress?"

AK. "Yes."

F.   "Holding one's forehead is nature's way of dealing with stress. Is it all right if I hold your forehead to help you release your stress?"

AK.   "Yes, that would be all right."

One hand was cupped and placed gently on her forehead. The other was placed behind her head to support and to counter the pressure on her forehead.

F.   "AK, imagine that you can go back in time. You are at the point of birth. You have been listening to the thoughts of everyone around you, and watching what they are doing. You have become fearful, thinking that life would be much worse than expected. Now I want you to talk to yourself. You can talk out loud or quietly in your mind. Tell yourself with emotion, **'This is exactly what Heavenly Father showed me. I accepted it then, and I accept it now. What a wonderful opportunity for growth.'"**

There was a short pause, then she nodded her head to indicate that she was finished. The facilitator then had her repeat the same exercise two more times.

F.   "AK, imagine that somewhere deep within you there is a cloud of dark negative energy associated with fear, especially the fear of failure and the fear of mortality.

Now take two or three deep breaths. As you inhale, imagine that you are inhaling light. As you exhale, imagine that you are exhaling all the darkness and fear."

They paused while she took three deep breaths, after which she seemed much more calm and relaxed. The facilitator had her think about birth while he tested. This time the arm locked very firmly indicating that the stress associated with birth was gone.

F.	"AK, please come back to present time." (A firm test indicated that she was at present time.)

An age regression revealed that there was a problem lasting from age five to age ten.

F.	"AK, there seems to be an ongoing problem that lasted from age five to age ten. Do you have any memories associated with that period of time?"

AK.	"I have very few memories of my childhood."

F.	"Is there anyplace, or anyone associated with your childhood that cause you to feel fearful or uneasy in any way?"

AK.	"We lived next door to my grandparents. I never felt comfortable going over there. I remember not wanting to go, even when there was some family event at their home.”

F.   Testing as follows: "Think of fear, hold.” (Test, weak). "Pain, hold.” (Test, weak). "Abuse, hold” (Test, weak). "Sexual abuse, hold.” (Test, weak). "Ritual abuse, hold.” (Test, weak).

"AK, your spirit is indicating that you were sexually abused. That abuse was apparently connected to satanic ritual. Do you have any vague memories of such abuse?”

AK.   "I don’t remember any abuse.” (There was a pause while she thinks about the past.) "I have some vague memories of people in black capes chanting some strange words and doing something with candles.”

At this point the facilitator opened my book, "Healing The Inner Self,” to the chapter on Satanic Abuse and discussed briefly the effects of Satanism on the victim, going through each of the effects of Satanism as presented in that book.   This gave both AK and her spirit the necessary background so that they could do some meaningful testing.

F.   "AK, at this time do you have any of those effects of Satanism that we just discussed affecting you?” (Test, yes). "Do you have most, if not all of the listed possible effects of Satanism?” (Test, yes).

"At the end of World War II the US government brought to the United States many of the top German scientists. One of these was named Dr. Greenbaum. Dr. Greenbaum had been working on research in the field of mind control. The techniques he used were in many respects the same as those used in satanic ritual. He was financed by the United States to further his studies. One could say he took satanic ritual to deeper levels of control. Those who are involved in satanic ritual have adapted the techniques he used. As a result, victims often have multilayered programming along with multilayered implants. Because of this type of ritual abuse, conventional therapy often requires a long tedious approach to healing, one layer at a time. We need to find out if you have any of that multilayered programming."

" The different layers of programming are usually designated by Greek letters."

While testing the facilitator asked, "Are you programmed on the Alpha level?" (Test, yes). "Are you programmed on the Beta level?" (Test, yes). "The Gamma level?" (Test, yes). "Delta?" (Test, yes). "Theta?" (Test, no). "Omega?" (Test, yes).

"AK, you have been programmed on five out of six of the possible layers just tested."

"We have already mentioned the possibility of implants and found that you do have implants. There is a special kind of implant that acts like a spiritual computer. You can have several of these computers, each with its own separate program. These programs are there to control you. The computers are generally designated by a basic color. By designating them that way, your handler, the one who controls you, can activate any computer and its program at will."

He tested while asking, "AK, do you have a red computer implanted within you?" (Test, yes). "Do you have an orange one?" (Test, yes). "Yellow?" (Test, yes). "Green?" (Test, yes). "Blue?" (Test, yes). "Violet?" (Test, no). "Black?" (Test, no). "White?" (Test, yes).

"AK, you have six out of the eight that we tested. It is no wonder you are having the problems you have been experiencing. It's time to do something about the past. It is time to give those problems to the Savior and make the atonement of Jesus Christ effective in your life." The facilitator tested while asking, "Were you ritualized in your grandparents' home?" (Test, yes).

F.   "Do you believe that God, your Heavenly Father, knew all things from the beginning?"

AK.   "Yes, he knows all things."

F.   "Before you were born, did He know that you would be the victim of satanic ritual?"

AK.   "Yes, He must have known."

F.   "I believe that He is a very kind and loving Father. I don't believe that He would send you to earth knowing about the abuse without providing you with a way to heal. I believe that he provided you with a healing program, programmed permanently into your spirit."

Using kinesiology the facilitator asked her spirit the following question. "Did your Heavenly Father provide you with a healing program or process, permanently programmed into your spirit, a program that would heal you from all effects of satanic ritual?" (Test, yes).

F.   "Let us activate that healing program and eliminate all the effects of satanic ritual. Please raise your arm to the square and repeat out loud after me."

AK.   **"In the name of Jesus Christ, I petition my Heavenly Father. Please activate the healing program within me, healing me on all levels. Let this healing program remove every effect of satanic ritual.**

In the name of Jesus Christ I command that all effects of satanic ritual be null and void. I command that all programs and their back-ups on all levels be canceled and deleted. I dismiss all effects of satanic ritual and cancel them out along with every spirit, thought form, energy, program, and residue associated with them. Cancel, cancel, cancel, and forever cancel." (She taps her chest in the middle about two inches below her collarbone while she says cancel; then holds the navel with the palm of her hand while she says forever cancel.)

F.   "Sometimes the implants, shunts, weapons and tools need a separate approach. To get rid of them, raise your arm to the square again and repeat the following after me."

AK.   **"In the name of Jesus Christ, I petition my Heavenly Father. Please send surgeons from the realm of light to surgically remove all implants including all spiritual computers, all weapons, tools, shunts, and anything else of that nature that remains with me. Then immediately heal the wounds that are left in my spirit. I accept that healing with praise, love and gratitude. Accept, accept, accept, forever with me."** (She taps her chest about two inches below her collarbone while she says accept. She then holds the navel with the palm of her hand while she says forever with me.)

F.   "We have created a void that needs to be filled. Again raise your arm to the square and repeat after me."

AK.   **"In the name of Jesus Christ I petition my Heavenly Father. Please fill the void within me by giving me at this time every positive spiritual gift, intelligence, light, and anything else that I need to**

help me accomplish my life's mission.   Accept, accept, accept.   Forever with me"

The facilitator retested the stress level and found it to be near zero.   He then asked while testing, "Is there anything else that we can or should do today." (Test, no).

F.   "When one finds satanic ritual, and then goes through the clearing process as we have done, there is always the possibility of having the victim of ritual confront the perpetrators.   This can case some real problems.   It could even result in a lawsuit.   In such cases the perpetrator will usually defend his position by claiming that the victim has "false memories created by the therapist."   For that reason it is wise for one to protect oneself.   The best protection is just to release the abuse and go on with your life saying nothing."

"There is no guarantee that kinesiology is 100% accurate.   The answers we got are based upon the perceptions of your spirit.   There are many ways that we can have memories that seem very real when in fact they are not real memories of our own past.   For example a spirit or a fragment of a spirit when attached to a person can bring with it the memories of its own past.   Sometimes we accept those memories as our own, and even attach those memories to some real person of our past.   Such a memory is known as a false memory."

"When dealing with abuse of any kind, especially

sexual or ritual abuse, it is not important to know whether or not the abuse was real. A false memory can affect one as much as a real memory. The important thing is to release the effects of the memory and get on with your life. That process is called, 'making the atonement work.'"

"Sometimes people cling to the past thinking that they must know who did it, and place the blame on the perpetrator. Such a one is not allowing the atonement to be effective. When one lets go of the past and gives the burden to the Savior, the past truly does not matter except for what can be learned. The best thing you can do at this time is to learn from the past and let it go. Don't cling to it by discussing it with others."

This finished the session.

Note: At the end of a session where one has discovered either sexual or ritual abuse, a discussion as given here is a very wise thing to do. It can save you from those who would like to accuse you of creating false memories.

7

DIVORCE

GF is a woman age 55. She was married for thirty years to the same man. Five years ago he announced to her that he had not loved her for a long time and he left.

GF had heard of kinesiology but was not familiar with it. The facilitator demonstrated how it works by testing after running the central meridian up, then again, after running it down. He then tested after asking, "Is your name GF?" A yes answer resulted in a very strong test, and a no answer resulted in a very weak test. She was ready to proceed.

Testing for being switched revealed no problem.

There was one chakra that was low in energy and that was easily taken care of.

She was tested to see if there were any devils or unclean spirits with her. The test revealed three unclean spirits but no devils. When the facilitator talked to them about going to the light, two of them left very quickly. One of the spirits was still present. He suspected that she had nested spirits. This proved to be true. To release them

132

they went through the process as described on page 191 entitled "Nested Spirits." They left very easily and quickly. Everything progressed exactly as described in that section.

F.   "As we go through life, every experience leaves a residue. This residue could be described as energy, or as a vibration. This residue can be either positive or negative. When Christ asked us to cast our burdens upon him, it was that residue of negative energy that Christ was asking for."

"Literally speaking, we cannot give Christ our sins. Once a sin is committed it is history. We cannot change history. Therefore, we cannot give Christ that event. We can, however, give him the negative residue. The negative residue that troubles us comes from every negative experience of life. Our own personal sins account for only a small portion of that residue. Christ asked us to cast all of our burdens upon him, not just those burdens associated with our personal sins."

"Let us now measure how much darkness you have accumulated throughout your life. We will measure it on a scale of zero to one hundred. One hundred is the maximum amount anyone could ever have, because that would bring them to the point of death."

They next did a stress test and found her stress level to be 63 on a scale of zero to one hundred.

F.   "GF, I would like to help you find the source of

your stress. We will find it by starting at your present age and counting backward. When we get to the age when something happened that your spirit wants to deal with first, the arm will unlock." The age regression revealed a problem at age 50.

F.   "What happened five years ago?"

GF.   "That was a very difficult time in my life. My husband and I were having a little argument. He blurted out, 'I haven't loved you for a long time.' He then packed his things and moved out and we were soon divorced."

F.   "GF, think of the word 'guilt.'" (Test, weak). "Are you blaming yourself for the divorce?"

GF.   "We were married for 30 years. We did have our problems, but I never expected our marriage to end in divorce. I'm sure there are things I could have done differently. Maybe it is my fault."

F.   "Do you see yourself as being responsible for the divorce?" (Test, yes).

     "It is easy for one to hold to the past and blame oneself. By doing so, you keep yourself filled with darkness. It is time for you to let go. Clinging to negative memories and thinking about 'what might have been' is very destructive. It is time to learn what you can from the past, and move on."

"When you hold your forehead gently with a cupped hand, you give your body bio-feed-back that causes the body to produce very positive body chemistry. This helps you to deal with stress. Would you please do that now while you repeat after me?"

GF. GF holds her forehead while repeating after the facilitator. **"The past is over and it doesn't matter any more except for what we can learn from it. I release the past and I forgive myself for my part in the divorce."** She repeated this about three times.

F. "GF, imagine that you have an open conduit right into heaven. Through that conduit send a prayer to Heavenly Father. You can pray quietly in your mind and in your own words. Thank Heavenly Father for allowing you to go through that trial. Ask Him to inspire you and teach you, helping you to learn everything you can learn from that experience, so that the experience will not be wasted."

There is a short pause as she processes, then she gives me a nod.

F. "Now GF, once again think of the divorce and your part in it. Now think of the word guilt." (Test, strong). "That is a lot better. Now think of the word rejection."

(Test, weak). "It seems as though you have let go of the guilt, but you are still dealing with a great deal of rejection. Do you think that is true?"

GF. "Yes, it sure is. I have never gotten over it. Even though our marriage was not the best, when he left it was totally unexpected, and I really felt rejected. Rejection seems to be a pattern of my life."

F. "Do you believe that there is opposition in all things?"

GF. "Yes, I do."

F. "Inasmuch as there really is opposition in all things, just as surely as there are spiritual gifts that come from the Holy Spirit, there are also negative spiritual gifts that come from Satan. Positive spiritual gifts increase our ability to perform in a positive way. Negative spiritual gifts increase our ability to perform in a negative way. I would like to search for the negative spiritual gifts that have impacted your life. To do this, I will name the possible negative spiritual gifts while testing. If the gift is present, your arm will test weak. If there is no problem, your arm will test very strong."

The facilitator went through quite a list of negative gifts and found the following ones to be present: rejection, guilt, fear of failure, doubt, control, and low self esteem.

F.   "My favorite scripture says that having faith in Jesus Christ, we can command in His name and do all things. We can use that principle to get rid of those negative gifts. All we need to do is command them to depart. We will do this in the name of Jesus Christ. You can add power to that command by raising your arm to the square. Please repeat after me."

GF.   While holding her arm to the square she repeated the following: **"In the name of Jesus Christ I command that all negative spiritual gifts depart. I dismiss them without argument and cancel them out along with every spirit, thought form, energy, and residue associated with them. Cancel, cancel, cancel, forever cancel."**

While saying, "cancel," she tapped the chest over the thymus. While saying, "Forever cancel" she held the navel with the palm of one hand

F.   "By sending those negative spiritual gifts away, we have created a void that must be filled. To do this, we need all the power we can get. Please raise your arm to the square and repeat after me."

GF.   **"In the name of Jesus Christ I petition my Heavenly Father. Please fill the void within me by giving me at this time every positive spiritual gift,**

intelligence, light, and anything else that I need to help me accomplish my life's mission. Accept, accept, accept, forever with me."

While saying, "accept," she tapped the chest over the thymus and while saying, "For ver with me," she held the navel with the palm of one hand.

A follow up test showed that all negative gifts were gone, and the void had been filled.

F.   "Up to this point we have been working primarily with the spirit.   You might have some negative programming in the physical body. The programming that we need to be most concerned about would be programming that would make you feel rejected, guilty, and have low self-esteem. We need to measure such programming. On a scale of zero to ten how bad is such programming in your physical nature."   (A test showed that she was at a nine.)

GF went through the brain gym and the EFT tapping sequence as given in the appendage at the back of the book. After which a retest showed her to be at a level zero.

Further testing indicated that we had dealt with as much as she could handle in one session, and that we were finished.

Note: There is a great benefit achieved by having the client thank the Lord for their trial. To begin with, the client only sees the trial as a terrible dark burden, an experience that is looked upon with negative emotion. When one thanks the Lord for such a trial the client's perspective is completely changed. The trial suddenly becomes an opportunity for growth. Such a prayer is an important part of the healing process.

8

SAME SEX ATTRACTION

LK is a woman age 48. She is a very successful attorney and is married. She was very knowledgeable about kinesiology muscle testing and it was very easily to get good accurate answers to the tests.

Testing revealed that she was not switched, and that her chakras were open and flowing properly.

A test revealed that she had two spirits with her. Further testing indicated that they were both earth bound spirits of people who had lived and died. When I told her that she had two spirits with her she asked, "Are they male or female?"

F.   "Why do you ask?"

LK.   "I have read your book, and I paid special attention to the chapter on "Same Sex Attraction." Although I have never acted on it, this has been an issue in my life. It isn't a constant problem. It is a problem that seems to come and go. I am married and I usually have no problem with sex.

In fact, I usually enjoy it very much but there have been times when I have known women whom I have found myself attracted to. The problem has been great enough to cause me some real concern. I mentioned it to my husband and that really caused some problems with him."

F.   While testing he asked, "are both of these spirits male?" (Test, yes). "Well, that explains the problem. I suppose that you have a very strong personality and you are able to override their influence most of the time, but from time to time they have been able to influence your sexual preference."

As the facilitator worked with these spirits, he taught them how to go to the light. One left rather quickly. The other one seemed to be more stubborn. The stubborn one turned out to be nested spirits with four spirits all of whom were male. By following the procedure given in the appendage for nested spirits, they all left rather quickly.

F.   "LK, sometimes spirits come at the time of birth. Birth is probably very painful and pain weakens our energy field, or in other words our shield of protection. When that energy field is weakened, the spirits can come in. In such a case we tend to accept such spirits along with our new body as part of us, and we do not recognize them as foreign entities. Instead of recognizing them as what they truly are, we accept them as a bundle of spiritual gifts and try to make them part of us."

"These spirits are usually well meaning spirits. They think they are contributing to us, even to the point of believing that they are the source of some of our spiritual gifts. In reality, they do not contribute anything positive. Instead, they bring darkness into us and cause problems. I would like your spirit to take inventory of every aspect of your being. Look carefully. Do you have any such spirits with you?" (Test, yes).

They asked, using kinesiology, and found that two out of three of those spirits were male.

F.   "LK, talk to these spirits. You can either talk out loud, or you can talk to them in your mind. Tell them, **'Now that I know that you are really not a part of me, I apologize for clinging to you and bonding to you. I release you. You are free to go to the light. Please go to the light just as the others did.'"**

There was a short pause while LK talked to them quietly in her mind. A test that followed showed that they were gone. They then filled the void as discussed in the appendage.

LK.   "What about the concept taught by those who claim to be experts in the field? They claim that a gay person is born that way."

F.   "Sometimes the spirit of the opposite sex, that causes the person to have the same sex attraction, comes at the time of birth. That spirit can influence one during one's entire life. In such a case the person really was born that way, but the problem need not be permanent. It comes from the foreign entity and when that spirit is sent away, the problem is gone."

"How do you feel? Is there any noticeable difference now that those spirits are gone?"

LK.   "I have never felt so full of light. I feel more at peace and more complete than I can remember ever feeling. I feel more feminine. This is really wonderful. I didn't think it would make this much difference."

The facilitator tried to proceed through the suggested sequence but none of the test revealed any other issues that could be dealt with.

F.   "Up to this point we have been primarily working with healing the spirit. You may have some programming in your physical nature that contributes to the problem. I am asking your spirit to examine your physical nature. On a scale of zero to ten, how bad is the programming that contributes to the problem of same sex attraction?"

The facilitator tested as he went through the numbers starting at zero. All numbers resulted in a strong test until the number four. That was high enough to be significant, but it was also consistent with the fact that the problem was not an everyday ongoing problem.

LK went through the brain gym and the EFT tapping sequence as given in the appendage. A retest showed the programming to be at the zero level.

LK had no other problems that she wanted to address. She went away feeling that the session was a total success.

Note: In dealing with the problem of same sex attraction I have found that with some people once the spirits leave there is no recurrence of the problem. With other people it seems as if they attract the spirits that cause the problem. In such cases, I have found that if one is vigilant in keeping the spirits away, the one who has been troubled with the problem can lead a very normal life.

9

A GREATLY FRAGMENTED SPIRIT

JJ is a woman in her early fifties. She has been going to a therapist for several years. She and her therapist are both aware of the fact that she is badly fragmented, having hundreds of personalities. A very concerned friend brought her to a facilitator. In their first encounter she was wary, not knowing what to expect. He took some time explaining some of the basic concepts that he works with, then demonstrated kinesiology. He was able to get a good test and she cautiously agreed to proceed.

Testing showed that she was switched. This was quickly corrected.

When her chakras were tested it was found that there was one chakra that was not functioning properly. This was corrected as discussed in the first section of the book.

Testing revealed the presence of two spirits. They were not very powerful and were easily sent to the light.

The facilitator did a stress test that revealed a very

high level of stress.

In doing an age regression, she immediately went back to age eighteen months. She indicated that at that time her father and his friends sexually abused her. This abuse was very intense and it continued until she was in her early teen years.

This ongoing abuse had caused her spirit to fragment into hundreds of separate personalities. She referred to them as alters.

The facilitator suggested that JJ visualize herself in a very peaceful meadow. She then invited all these separate alters to join her there.

F.   "JJ, call these alters together and bless them with light and love. Imagine bright light surrounding them, filling them with love and peace. Invite the Savior to come into the meadow with them. Now imagine the Savior giving them a blessing. As the darkness is replaced with light, you will see them dance for joy and they will hug each other. As two of them hug each other, you will see them join and blend into one. As they connect and blend, the number of alters will gradually become smaller and smaller."

There was a pause of a minute or more during which she commented from time to time that the number of alters was decreasing. They seem to have reached a stable number of about fifty.

F.   "JJ, this will take a little time, but I need you to go
to each one of them, one at a time. Take both of their
hands into yours, look into their eyes and tell them, 'I love
you. I have missed you, and I need you. You need me. It
is time to heal. As they look into your eyes they will access
your memory and will become fully aware of every event of
your life. When you are ready, give that little one a big hug
and she will step inside of you, becoming part of you
again."

Because there were so many of them, it took what
seemed like a long time for her to connect with each one,
but finally she announced that they were all back with her.
There was no one in the meadow but her.

Because this work was so new to her, JJ was
unwilling to do anything else at that time. She did,
however, attend my seminar the next day. The next
contact JJ had with the facilitator was about three weeks
later. At that time he was unable to have a session with her
but they did have time to visit. She was very disturbed.
She was so different from how she had been, she did not
know herself. She felt that she was incomplete and alone
because she could not find her other alters. The facilitator
tried to explain to her that she had not lost anything.
Those alters were not lost, but rather, they were now a part
of her and she was more complete. She made an
appointment for a follow-up session.

In the follow-up session JJ was really ready and open. It was found that she had not forgiven her father or his friends who had abused her. She went through the process of forgiving them, and then offering to them all the healing that is available through Christ. She released them to the Savior, and visualized the light and love of Christ completely cleansing her.

JJ still felt incomplete, and as she and the facilitator discussed it she indicated that she felt that her core personality was not present, and that one of her alters was in charge. They found the core personality. It seemed to be a young girl of about thirteen. They visited with the core personality and blessed her with light. She very willingly came back and the alter that had been substituting for her was fully integrated into her spirit.

JJ now feels complete. She commented several times about how complete and whole she felt. She commented on the silence in her head that allowed her to hear sounds such as the birds that were outside the window. She felt that she was full of light, and even the room seemed to be filled with heavenly light.

I must add to this the following: JJ is having some difficulty adjusting. She is so used to all her alters being present that being just one personality is very new to her and very different. She feels bad because, "She has to do all the work. She can't assign jobs to her various alters." I bring out this fact because healing can be painful and it often takes effort, but it is worth every bit of the required work.

Note: This is another good example that illustrates that although a facilitator may try to follow the suggested sequence, the client and the client's spirit are in charge of the session and the facilitator must skip to what ever step of the sequence the client needs.

10

REBELLIOUS DEVILS

PP is a woman in her mid forties. She has had quite a number of sessions because she was deeply programmed in satanic ritual. She has been one who could not process everything at once. She had to release the programming one layer at a time.

As in the case of most people who have been the victim of satanic ritual, she had a very fragmented spirit and manifested many personalities which she referred to as alters.

After the first few sessions, most of the time, the sessions with her consisted of getting rid of two or three spirits and then finding a few alters that were ready to be integrated.

The spirits that came with her were nearly always the kind we refer to as devils. Usually it would take about twenty minutes to convince them that they could go to the light. Once they could accept that concept they usually went willingly, and then PP and the facilitator could proceed with the session.

At the beginning of one recent session, PP walked into the facilitator's office and sat down. Before he could say anything she looked at him with a look in her eye that let him know that there was a devil in charge. She began to speak. Her voice was low and unnatural. This is what followed:

Spirit. (The spirit speaking through PP): "Before you do anything, let us tell you our position."

F.   "Go ahead, I'll listen. What is your position?"

Spirit. "There are two of us here. Satan asked for two volunteers to come with her to keep her from healing. We volunteered. We did not volunteer because we wanted to please Satan. We are sick and tired of him and we want to be free. We know that most of the spirits who come into your office end up going to the light. We want you to teach us how."

"We are not alone. There is a great undercurrent of dissatisfaction within Satan's hosts. There are legions of his followers who also want out. We are simply the vanguard who has come to be taught. When you teach us, you will also be teaching the others. They are gathered in front of your office. They can see and they can hear. As you teach us, you will be teaching them."

F.   "How many are there?"

Spirit. "There are about two million. As you teach us, you will be teaching all of them."

F.   "All of you are children of God. He is your Heavenly Father, and He loves you very much. Jesus Christ is your brother, and he also loves you very much. Heavenly Father and Jesus Christ are anxious for you to return to their presence and dwell in light where you can once again be in a state of eternal progression. All you need to do is look up and cry out to Christ, saying, 'I was deceived. Please forgive me. I want to come back.'"

Spirit. "Is that all there is to it?"

F.   "Yes, that is all there is to it. You will be welcomed back with open arms."

Spirit. "Thank you. Good by."

With that, they were gone, but that is not the end of the story. PP responded with quite a wonderful description of what she saw.

PP claimed that as the facilitator was talking with these two spirits, it seemed to her as if the front of his office suddenly disappeared. She was looking through the wall as if it didn't even exist. It looked like a great open plain with a huge army gathered together. They seemed to be innumerable. They were surrounded in a cloud of darkness. As the facilitator said, 'look up,' they all raised their arms toward heaven and suddenly the darkness was gone, and they were completely engulfed in beautiful heavenly light. Then, they began floating upward. She watched them until they all disappeared. Then suddenly the vision closed and again she saw the walls of the office as before.

As the facilitator took her through the suggested sequence, nothing came up until they checked for a fragmented spirit. There were still a few alters that were ready to come back. This session seemed to be the one that completely finished the process of healing PP from satanic ritual.

Note: On another occasion in a different city when I was away from home, I had an almost identical experience with another woman.

11

CHILDREN

LF is a middle-aged woman. She has a friend who comes to visit with her about once a week. The friend usually stays for about an hour. The friend is pleasant and the visit would be good except for the fact that the friend always brings her little preschool boy, Jeff. LF has a toy box for children like Jeff, but Jeff is not a normal little boy. After an hour visit the toys are everywhere and the house is in a mess.

One day LF was thinking about Jeff and it occurred to her that Jeff is probably the way he is because of spirits that are attached to him. The next time Jeff's mother came to visit, LF went over to Jeff and said, "Jeff, it is good to have you here. Let me give you a little hug." As she hugged Jeff she talked quietly in her mind to the spirits who were with him. She asked the spirits to give their burdens to Christ, and then commanded them to leave.

That day when Jeff's mother was ready to leave Jeff said, "Wait mom, I need to pick up the toys. When they left the house was neat and orderly. After that, there was no problem with Jeff.

CJ is a five-year-old boy who liked to play with matches. His mother contacted a facilitator by phone one day. She was very fearful and wanted to know if there was anything he could do to solve the problem. CJ had just been playing with matches and had created a situation that could have caused a house fire had the mother not been as alert as she was at that time.

Using a surrogate the facilitator tested CJ and found that he did have a spirit with him. Using kinesiology, he asked this spirit, "when you lived upon the earth with a body of your own, were you greatly involved with fire?" (Test, yes).

Even though CJ was many miles away, the facilitator knew that he could talk to the spirit in his mind. Spirits communicate by thought transfer and distance does not make any difference. He talked to the spirit and instructed him, telling him how he could go to the light. Using the surrogate again he tested and found that the spirit was gone.

He followed up later with CJ's mother and found that he no longer had any desire to play with matches.

BD is a delightful little four-year-old boy. His mother was concerned because he often showed an interest in female clothes and toys. Using a surrogate a test revealed that he had a female spirit with him. Sending that spirit to the light was like flipping a switch. He suddenly started playing with trucks and other boy toys.

Recently BD's mother called and said, "BD must have another visitor. I went shopping today and he was having a fit because I wouldn't get him a cute little pink girls purse." This is not the first time this has happened. Each time the facilitator gets a phone call like that one, he pauses just long enough to talk to the spirits that are with BD. He sends them to the light, and immediately his mother reports that BD is once again attracted to boy things.

Some little boys seem to attract the female spirits more than the male ones. I have found, however, that if you are alert to the problem and keep sending the spirits away, these little boys can grow up quite normally.

DF is a little boy in the third grade. He has been a concern, not only to his parents, but also to the teachers and school administrators. He has often grabbed little girls on the playground and then pulled their panties down. When a little boy his age is doing things like that, one can't help but worry about what he will be doing when he is older.

A facilitator was in DF's home visiting with the parents. They told him of DF's behavior and their concerns.

He called DF into the room and asked him if he could "play a game with him." He did a muscle test finding it to be very strong for a little boy. He then ran his central meridian backward and tested. Of course it was weak. He was surprised. They made a fun game out of it. The facilitator then tested for spirits and found several. He did not tell DF he had spirits. He only said that he had some negative energy that needed to be eliminated. He worked with the spirits in his mind.

A retest showed them to be gone. They did nothing else at that time. Later the facilitator followed up with the parents. It has been more than a year, and during the time since they were together, there has been no reoccurrence of the problem.

12

PANIC ATTACKS

GW is a forty-four year-old woman. She has been involved in several forms of natural healing and was very knowledgeable in regards to kinesiology. This made her very easy to work with. It was very easy to get good answers to the testing.

The facilitator asked GW if she had any particular concerns that she wanted to address. She indicated that from time to time she had difficulty with depression and panic attacks. Her panic attacks were not the kind that come and go, but rather became a lingering fear and dread.

The facilitator checked to make sure there was no problem of being switched and that the chakras were open and functioning correctly. He then tested for the presence of spirits.

Through testing, it was found that she had three earthbound spirits with her. These spirits were very easily sent to the light.

The facilitator asked her spirit if those spirits had been a major contributing factor in her panic attacks.

(Test, yes).

They did a stress test that revealed her stress level to be at 63. They then did an age regression to see where that stress came from and found a problem at age two. She had no memory of that part of her life, so it became necessary for them to test key words to find the original problem.

They tested words such as father, mother, sister, and neighbor. The word neighbor resulted in a weak test. They then tested other words such as fear, anger, pain, and abuse. The words that gave a negative response were fear and pain.

Putting the word neighbor together with fear and pain brought them to the conclusion that there was some experience at age two involving the neighbor, possibly a minor incident. While testing the facilitator asked if there was some minor incident that, although it was not serious from a health and safety point of view, did cause fear and pain. (Test, yes).

The facilitator helped GW go through the process of visualizing the neighbor, then forgiving him and releasing him. She did not know who the neighbor was, so she did not put a face or a name on him.

She then imagined light coming into her body flushing out and replacing all the energy of fear. Testing revealed that there was no longer any sadness or negative energy associated with the word neighbor. That was a big step in the right direction, but the word fear still yielded a very weak test.

Sometimes you have to just keep digging until you find what you are looking for. This was one of those cases. The facilitator went to the next step in the suggested sequence that being negative spiritual gifts. They found that she had negative gifts of fear, anger, doubt, and depression. Testing also revealed that Satan was able to slip these gifts in at age two when she was dealing with fear and pain.

GW raised her arm to the square and repeated the following; **"In the name of Jesus Christ I command that all negative spiritual gifts depart. I dismiss them without argument and cancel them out along with every spirit, thought form, energy, and residue associated with them. Cancel, Cancel, Cancel. Forever cancel."**

She then filled the void by again raising her arm to the square and repeating the following, **"In the name of Jesus Christ I petition my Heavenly Father. Please fill the void within me by giving me at this time every positive spiritual gift, intelligence, light, and anything else that I need to help me accomplish my life's mission."**

It was explained that up to this point they had been primarily dealing with the spirit. The facilitator suggested that the negative thoughts and patterns associated with those negative gifts were also programmed into the physical nature. By testing on a scale of zero to ten, that programming was found to be an eight. After going through the brain gym and the tapping sequence as found in the appendage at the back of the book, a retest showed the programming to be at a level zero.

Proceeding with the suggested sequence the facilitator tested for fragmentation of the spirit, phobias, and ritual abuse. None of these tests revealed any additional problems.

At this point they again tested the stress level and found it to be a one on a scale of zero to one hundred.

They were finished.

13

GENERATIONAL ISSUES

GR is a woman in her sixties. She was raised in a family where the father was very abusive and controlling. Her mother was badly abused. There was evidence that her mother was the victim of sexual abuse when she was a child.

GR is very gifted spiritually and often reports feeling the presence of various deceased family members with her.

GR came for a session after having had sessions before. She was familiar with the techniques described in the next section of the book entitled "Repatterning – Specific Approach," and she requested that in this session she wanted to go through that process to see what she could uncover and release.

They first checked to make sure there were no spirits attached to her then immediately went through the repatterning process.

As they got to step three of that process she became very emotional and indicated that she could feel her deceased mother there with her. She also very strongly felt that the negative patterns that were being brought forward were patterns that applied to her mother more than they did to her.

As they finished the session, GR reported that her mother thanked her and left.

They both felt that the "Repatterning" technique is not only effective in dealing with one's own issues, it is a very effective technique for releasing generational issues.

Note: In section three of this book there are a few techniques that are not normally included in the suggested sequence. These techniques can be very helpful when doing follow-up sessions when you are dealing with specific issues or situations, with no intention of going through the normal suggested sequence. This case was one of those.

14

HEALING EIGHT
GENERATIONS

JC is a man in his mid fifties. He and his wife SC
came together and the facilitator worked with both of them.
SC is very gifted spiritually and reported that she could see
spirits. This made for a very interesting session because as
he worked with JC, SC made comments as to how his
guardian angels reacted during the session.

They both had had sessions before and were very
familiar with the techniques discussed in my book. On this
particular day, they started in the usual manner. The
facilitator made sure that the testing was giving clear
answers. They then checked for being switched and
checked the chakras. There were no problems.

They then checked to make sure there were no
spirit attachments. The test indicated that there was one
spirit with JC. The spirit was sent to the light rather easily.

A stress test indicated that on a scale of zero to one
hundred, JC had a stress level in the low forties.

An age regression took JC back to his early

164

childhood. When the facilitator ask JC if he had any memories of negativity associated with that period of his life, nothing came to mind, so they started probing. They tested key words such as father, mother, brother, and sister. When testing "father" the test was very weak. They then tested words such as fear, rejection, anger, abuse, and sexual abuse. "Abuse" resulted in a weak test, and "sexual abuse" was even weaker.

JC became very emotional and recounted situations of abuse wherein his father had abused him. They proceeded as follows:

F.   "JC, the way to release the negative emotional residue associated with that abuse is to forgive. Are you ready to forgive your father?"

JC.   "Oh yes. I don't want to cling to that any more."

F.   "Close your eyes and get a picture of your father in your mind. Now go through the following steps. You can do it out loud or in your mind. If you do it silently in your mind just give me a little nod to let me know when you are finished."

"In your own words, adding all the detail you wish to add, first tell your father that you love him. Next tell him that the past is over and doesn't matter anymore except for what can be learned from it, and then, from your heart, tell your father that you forgive him. Forgive him of everything he ever said or did that offended you. Forgive him of everything he didn't say or do that offended you. Ask him to forgive you of anything you did that offended him in any way. Last of all tell him once again that you love him."

There was a pause while JC processed it quietly in his mind. He then gave me a nod.

F.   "Now go through it again."

Again there was a pause while JC processed it in his mind.

JC.   "I have such a feeling of release. I feel like I just lifted a great burden from my shoulders.

At this point SC, his wife, spoke up. "I saw JC's deceased father come into the room. As JC forgave his father, his father bowed in an attitude of appreciation and said, 'Now that I have been forgiven I can progress.' Immediately JC's grandfather came into the room and JC's father forgave his own father for abuse he had received as a child. Grandfather then bowed in an attitude of appreciation just as JC's father had done and said, 'Now that I have been forgiven, I can progress.'"

SC said that she counted while this pattern kept repeating over and over, and the generational abuse was forgiven and released back eight generations.

A test indicated that JC had negative spiritual gifts of low self-esteem, doubt, and control. These were released and the void was filled.

Testing indicated no sign of fragmentation, phobias or ritual abuse.

Testing to see if there was negative programming in his physical nature that needed to be released by EFT showed that on a scale of zero to ten he was an eight. The EFT tapping sequence brought that down to zero and they were finished.

15

ALLERGIC TO HORSES

JB is a young boy in his early teens. His mother came for a session. As they finished she asked, "My son JB is allergic to horses. Is there anything you can do to help him? I came from a family of ranchers. We visit the family ranch quite often, and when we do, we all like to go horseback riding. Up until about a year or two ago JB enjoyed the horses right along with the rest of us, but now he can't ride with us any more because he has become allergic to the horses."

F.   "As you know, I don't treat specific health problems that is not my field. It is true, however, that many illness seem to come as a result of the presence of spirits, or some underlying emotional condition. That I can deal with. Let's see what can be done."

JB was not familiar with kinesiology and as he was introduced to it his reaction was one of amazement. He accepted it very quickly and they were ready to proceed.

A test showed that there was no problem with being switched, but when the chakras were tested it was found that one chakra was not flowing properly. This was corrected very quickly and they were ready to proceed.

The facilitator tested JB and found that he had two spirits with him. Using kinesiology he asked some questions that were directed to those spirits. The answers he got indicated that one of those spirits was very much afraid of horses because during his life on earth he had been badly injured by a horse. The spirits were very easily released and sent to the light.

The facilitator next measured JB's stress level and found it to be in the low twenties. This was not very high; however, it is a significant level.

An age regression revealed that there was an incident about two years ago while riding horses that caused JB to have some fear of horses. JB thought about the incident for a moment then repeated the following:

JB. **"The past is over and it doesn't matter any more except for what can be learned. I release the past and give the incident to the Lord. It is safe for me to ride and enjoy horses."**

They next tested key words such as fear, anger, rejection, etc. The only word that produced a negative response was the word "fear."

F.   Asking with kinesiology, "Do you have a negative gift of fear? (Test, yes). "Do you have a negative gift of fear of horses?" (Test, yes).

F.   "JB, you need to release those gifts. Please raise your arm to the square and repeat after me:

JB.   While holding his arm to the square he repeated the following: **"In the name of Jesus Christ I command that all negative spiritual gifts depart, especially the gifts of fear and the fear of horses. I dismiss them without argument and cancel them out along with every spirit, thought form, energy, and residue associated with them. Cancel, (tap). Cancel, (tap). Cancel, (tap). Forever cancel."**

F.   "Up to this point we have been working on the healing of the inner self. The inner self seems to have completely released the issue. You probably still have some of the same programming in your physical self. We need to measure the amount of negative programming in the physical body."

They measured that negative programming on a scale of zero to ten, and found it to be at a level seven. They then went through the EFT tapping sequence as given in the next section of the book and then tested again. This time the test showed a level zero.

The facilitator then tested JB on each of the remaining items of the suggested sequence and found nothing.

This finished the session, and the facilitator has not seen JB since then but he has seen and talked to his mother several times. It has been over a year since this session with JB. JB's family has visited the family ranch several times and there has never been any indication of any allergy.

16

REJECTED BY PEERS

SW is a single parent who has been struggling with personal issues most of her life. A friend told her about my book, "Healing The Inner Self." After reading the book she called and made an appointment with a facilitator.

As they started, the facilitator asked what she hoped to accomplish during her session with him. She responded that she had been struggling with depression and low self-esteem since she was about twelve or thirteen.

She was familiar with kinesiology and the facilitator found that he could communicate directly with her spirit very quickly and easily.

She was switched, and this was quickly corrected.

Testing the chakras showed that they were all open and flowing properly.

Using kinesiology testing he found that she had three spirits with her. Because of her previous comment about struggling since the age of twelve or thirteen, using kinesiology, he asked how long these spirits had been with her. Two had come relatively recently, but one came at the age of twelve when her depression started.

The spirits all indicated that they were earthbound spirits of mortals who had in the past lived and died. Two of them left quickly, but one remained. The remaining spirit turned out to be more than just one spirit. It was a nest of spirits that was five deep. Using the technique for dealing with nested spirits as given on page 191, they were released and all of them seemed to go to the light.

They tested for spirits that may have come at the time of birth, and found two more spirits. These were easily released and sent to the light. This was done by having SW speak to them.

SW.   Repeating the following: **"Now that I know that you are not part of me I apologize for bonding to you and clinging to you. I release you. You are free to go to the light just as the others did."**

A test indicated that all of them immediately left. SW reported that she felt a significant difference.

F.   "These spirits have been with you all of your life, and they have become part of your comfort zone. Sending them away has created a void. If we do not do something to fill that void, you will feel as if you have lost your best friends. To fill that void I need you to raise your arm to the square and out loud repeat after me."

SW.   **"In the name of Jesus Christ I petition my Heavenly Father. Please fill the void within me by giving me at this time every positive spiritual gift, intelligence, light, and anything else that I need to help me accomplish my life's mission. Accept, accept, accept, forever with me"**

While saying, "accept" she tapped her chest in the middle about two inches below her collarbone. While saying "forever with me," she held her navel with the palm of her hand.

They measured her stress level and found it to be in the low sixties. Usually the facilitator immediately follows this by doing an age regression, but the still small voice within said, "Go directly to age twelve.

F.   "SW, what happened at age twelve that caused you emotional pain?

SW.   "Up to that point in my life, I felt that life was good. I had a number of good friends and was part of the group of popular kids. For no reason that I was aware of, some of the group started saying bad things about me. I couldn't figure out why they did it. I didn't try to defend myself. Instead, I withdrew. After that I continually dealt with depression and low self esteem."

F.   "Probably what was happening was that there were

some of the group who felt threatened by you. In any such group there is a 'pecking order.' These kids saw you as the leader of the group and they wanted to dethrone you and establish themselves as the leaders of the group. There was nothing wrong with you. The real problem was that you were a threat to them and they discredited you as a way of eliminating you from the group."

Using kinesiology testing the facilitator asked, "Is that what happened?" (Test, yes).

"It's time to forgive those former friends and release that issue of the past. Close your eyes and imagine that those who rejected you are here, then repeat out loud after me."

SW.   Repeating after the facilitator, using her own words, **"The past is over and it really doesn't matter any more. What really matters is what we can learn from the experiences of the past. I still love you and want you to have a good life. I forgive you for everything you ever said or did that offended me. I also forgive you for the things that you didn't say and didn't do that could have helped me. Forgive me for anything that I did that offended you. I really do love you."**

She was tested while thinking about those who had offended her. The test was really strong, indicating that those who had offended her were no longer a problem.

F.   "SW, because there is opposition in all things, inasmuch as the Lord can give positive spiritual gifts, it must be true that Satan has the power to give negative spiritual gifts. I am going to name some potential negative spiritual gifts. I will test after naming each gift. If you have that negative gift the arm will be weak. If not, it will be strong."

Many key words were tested. The tests indicated that she had the gifts of rejection, low self-esteem, fear, fear of failure, fear of success, doubt, control, hate, anger, and why try. These gifts were all related and it seemed logical that all of them could have come at the time she was being rejected by her friends.

F.   "SW, are you ready to release all of these negative gifts?

SW.   "Yes."

F.   "SW, so as to get all the power available to make this more effective, please raise your arm to the square and repeat after me."

SW.   Repeating after the facilitator, **"In the name of Jesus Christ I command that all negative spiritual gifts depart. I dismiss them without argument and cancel them out along with every spirit,**

thought form, energy, and residue associated with them. Cancel, cancel, cancel, forever cancel."

Again repeating as directed, **"In the name of Jesus Christ I petition my Heavenly Father. Please fill the void within me by giving me at this time every positive spiritual gift, intelligence, light, and anything else that I need to help me accomplish my life's mission. Accept, accept, accept, forever with me."**

F.   "Our spirits are composed of material called intelligence. Every part of our spirit is intelligent and you think with every part of your spirit. It is possible that when you were under great stress or pain, a part of your spirit said, 'I can't take this any longer.' And it left."

The facilitator asked while testing, "Are you missing any major fragments of you spirit? (Test, yes). Another test showed that only one fragment was missing.

F.   "SW, imagine that you are in a beautiful meadow enjoying the fresh air, sunshine, and the beautiful scenery. You see a young girl walk into the meadow. She looks just as you did at age twelve. And you realize that this young girl is a part of you. Tell her that the past is over and that it is time to heal from the negative events of the past. Tell her, 'I need you and you need me." SW repeated the above thoughts as directed but used her own words. As they continued SW blessed her younger self with light and love, then invited the Savior to come into the picture and give her a blessing.

Once SW's younger self had released all darkness and stress, SW was instructed to hold the hands of her younger self and look into her eyes. As she did so, the younger self downloaded the memory of everything she had missed out on. When they were ready the two SW's embraced and the younger self entered into the older and once again became part of a greater whole.

SW was instructed to take several deep breaths and while doing so, to imagine that she was inhaling light. That light was the glue needed to bind the two parts of the spirit together. This she did. A test that followed indicated that the process was complete and that the spirit fragments had become one completely integrated whole.

They tested to see if there were any missing small fragments, not big enough to have a personality of their own. (Test, yes)

F.   "SW, we all have guardian angels. They come at the time of birth and stay with us until the time of death. They are there to help us every way they can, but they do not interfere with out agency. Sometimes it helps to talk to them and give permission for them to help. Would you feel comfortable sending them out on a search and rescue mission?

SW.   "That sounds like a good idea. What do you have

in mind?

F.   "If you request their help, the Guardian angels will find every missing fragment of your spirit and return it. Just repeat after me."

SW.   Repeating after the facilitator, **"I am talking to my guardian angels. I authorize you to help me every way you can, so long as it does not interfere with the will of God. At this time I have a special mission for you.   Please find every missing fragment of my spirit. If any of them have been captured by anyone, demand their release. Cleanse each one. Heal each one and integrate them back into my spirit where they belong. I accept this healing with love, praise, and gratitude. Accept (tap), accept (tap), accept (tap), forever with me.** As she said accept she tapped her chest over the thymus gland (the middle of the chest about two inches below the collar bone). As she said forever with me she held the palm of her hand over her navel.

A test showed that all fragments of the spirit had returned.

Testing to see if there were any phobias or ritual abuse followed this. Nothing showed up at this time.

F.   "SW, up to this point we have been primarily

helping the spirit to heal. You may have negative programming within the physical body. This negative programming would be the counterpart of all the negative gifts and emotions that were eliminated. Let's measure the extent of that negative programming." We will do this on a scale of zero to ten. (A test showed a level eight.)

SW was directed through "Brain Gym" followed by the EFT tapping sequence" as given in the next session of the book.

Follow up tests showed the negative programming in the physical nature to be at a zero, and the stress level to also be at zero. They were finished.

About a month later there was a short follow-up by phone and it was reported that there was no more problem with depression and low self-esteem.

17

REJECTED AT BIRTH

BG is a 17 year-old girl who came with her mother and two other sisters. The mother had been to see the facilitator about three weeks prior and felt so much improvement in her own mental state that she wanted each of the children to have a private session.

They began as a group making sure that everyone understood kinesiology and when tested would give a good response.

They were checked for switching and the function of the chakras. They were corrected as needed.

They then checked for spirit attachments and found that everyone except the mother had at least two or three spirits attached. These spirits were quite easily sent to the light except for one that was attached to BG. That one turned out to be a nest of spirits and using the material on page 191 in the next section of the book entitled "Nested Spirits" they were quickly released.

They next checked each one to see if there were spirits that came at the time of birth. Each of the girls had two or three of this kind of spirit. They were all quickly released and sent to the light, and the void was filled.

At this point the facilitator started working with each one individually. BG was the oldest of the children and was the first one to take her turn. She chose to go into another room without other members of the family present.

A stress test showed her stress level to be in the high eighties. Because of that high stress level, it was evident that she had some real heavy issues that needed to be addressed.

When they did an age regression, she went immediately back to the time of birth.

F.   "BG, Are you aware of any problems associated with your birth?"

BG.   "Yes, my mother got pregnant before mom and dad got married. Dad wanted to have me aborted but mom would not consent."

F.   "Think of rejection."   (Test, weak)   "Think of father."   (Test, weak). ."Think of being rejected by your father." (Test, very weak).

"BG, what kind of relationship do you now have with your father?

BG.   "I've never been close to him. It just seems as if he is never there when I need him. He seems to have favorites and I am definitely not his favorite. He spends a lot more time with the other children than he does with me.

F.   "At this point I would like to walk you through the process of forgiving your father. To do this please hold your forehead gently with one hand, close your eyes, and get a picture of your father in your mind's eye. Then repeat after me. You can repeat out loud or quietly in your mind,"

BG.   Repeating after the facilitator out loud, **"Dad, the past is over. It really doesn't matter any more except for what we can learn from it. I love you very much and I forgive you for everything you ever said or did that offended me in any way. I forgive you for the things you didn't say or didn't do that offended me. Please forgive me for anything I have done that offended you in any way. I really love you and I thank you for everything you have done to help me."**

F.   "Now I want you to repeat all of that again, this time in your own words with one addition. While you go through that process imagine that there is a bright cord of light connecting your heart to your dad's heart. You can do this silently if you choose, but if you do, let me know when you are finished. You can give the signal that you are finished by taking a deep breath." She was directed to repeat that process twice.

Each time **BG** quietly went through the process of forgiving and releasing her father she ended with a big deep breath.

They did another age regression. This time the testing revealed that there was a major issue the previous year.

F.   "BG, what happened last year?

BG.   "Last year my very best friend moved. She moved all the way across the country, and although we have talked by phone and have written, I fear that I will never see her again. After she moved I was so depressed that I was hospitalized for a while."

F.   "Just as you did with your father, get a picture of your friend in your mind's eye. Tell her how much you love her. Tell her that you expect to see her again, but until you do, it is all right for both of you to let go and move on. Imagine that there are strings that connect the two of you. There should be one bright string of light that connects the two of you, heart to heart. That is a positive bond and is healthy. The other strings are negative bonds of control. Imagine that you have a large pair of scissors. Use them to cut all the strings of control. As you do so, tell her that you set her free." BG went through that exercise three times.

The facilitator spent a few minutes discussing the concept of negative spiritual gifts and then suggested that she probably has several of them. They checked by naming several of them as they tested. A weak test after naming a potential negative gift reveals its presence. It was found that she had a very strong negative gift of rejection. She also had a negative gift of low self-esteem, and a gift of fear of failure. To release these gifts BG raised her arm to the square and repeated the following:

BG. **"In the name of Jesus Christ I command that all negative spiritual gifts depart. I dismiss them without argument and cancel them out along with every spirit, thought form, energy, and residue associated with them. Cancel, cancel, cancel, forever cancel."**

While saying, "cancel," she taped the chest over the thymus, which is in the middle of the chest about two inches below the collarbone. While saying, "forever cancel," she held the navel with the palm of one hand.

A follow-up test shows that all negative spiritual gifts were gone.

LC. "By sending those negative gifts away, we have

created a void that needs to be filled. Raise your arm to the square again and repeat after me."

BG.   Repeating out loud after the facilitator, **"In the name of Jesus Christ I petition my Heavenly Father. Please fill the void within me by giving me at this time every positive spiritual gift, intelligence, light, and anything else that I need to help me accomplish my life's mission."**

The above was followed by having BG tap her chest in the middle about two inches below her collarbone while saying "accept, (tap), accept, (tap), accept, (tap)", then hold the navel with the palm of the hand and saying, "forever with me."

At this point they did a stress test and found the stress level to be at 20. That is a great improvement but it indicates that something more need to be done.

They tested to see if there was any fragmentation of the spirit. There was none.

F.   "Up to this point we have primarily been working on healing the inner self, or in other words, we have been healing the spirit.   You probably have negative programming in your physical body that must be released. That negative programming can be released by using a very simple technique."

"The Chinese teach that there are points on your body where you store the negative energy and programming. This can be neutralized and released by tapping those points. It helps if at the same time positive affirmations are repeated."

They tested to see how badly she was programmed in her physical body. On a scale of zero to ten, she was a nine. The facilitator walked BG through the brain gym sequence and the EFT tapping sequence as given in the next section of the book. Retesting to see the level of programming that remained followed, she was a one on a scale of zero to ten. That was not good enough. (I am never satisfied with any measurement other than zero.)

LC.   "BG, there is one more thing I would like to do at this point."

The facilitator again led BG through the Brain Gym sequence. He then had BG hold one hand in front of her face with the palm of the hand facing toward her face. With the fingers of the other hand she tapped the side of the hand between the wrist and the knuckle of the little finger. While BG was doing this, he drew a circle in front of her face with his finger, first rotating in one direction, then the other. She continued tapping the side of her hand and at the same time she focused her eyes on his finger. While all of this was going on, simultaneously she repeated

the affirmation found on the last page of the book, which is
as follows:

BG.   **"I am a child of God. Everything I am and
everything I do is a reflection of Him. Therefore, I
choose to glorify God. I deserve a good life. I
expect a good life. I claim a good life. I create a
good life. I have a good life which glorifies God
and demonstrates how a child of God should live."**

The facilitator switched to a sideways figure 8
motion with his finger in front of her, making sure that his
finger was moving in an upward direction when crossing
the midline of her body. At the same time BG repeated the
following:

BG.   "I have been dealing with a great deal of rejection,
low self-esteem, and a fear of failure. I give all of that to the
Savior." As she said I give all of that to the Savior the
facilitator gestured with his hand as if he were throwing
something over his shoulder.

He again returned to the sideways figure 8 motion
with his finger as before and had BG repeat the following
positive statement:

BG.   "I am accepted. I am loved. It is safe for me to be
who I am. Life is good and I accept it. I accept." As she

said, "I accept," the facilitator stopped the sideways figure 8 motion and with his finger pointed to her heart.

This was followed by going through the Brain Gym sequence once again.

The facilitator visited with BG for a few moments to see what her response would be. He wanted to know how she felt and whether or not she accepted the things that they had been doing. She said, "I feel light. In fact, I can't remember when I felt so good."

Using a scale of zero to ten, they tested the negative programming in her physical nature. The test showed the level to be zero. And testing on a scale of zero to one hundred, her stress level was also zero. The facilitator asked with kinesiology testing if there was anything else that could be done. The answer was no.

They were finished.

Note: For greater understanding of the last technique used with BG, I suggest that you turn to page 194 and read the section entitled "Repatterning – Specific Approach". This is one of those extra techniques listed in section three of the book, but not included in the regular suggested sequence.

SECTION THREE

ADDITIONAL HELPS

The material presented here in this section of the book consists of principles, techniques, and helps that are not included in my first book. Some of these principles and techniques are included in the suggested sequence giver in this book. Some are not included in my suggested sequence. These are included here to be used as the spirit directs, and they often help when all else fails.

Although the primary emphasis of the material I have presented, both in my first book and in this one, is the healing of the inner-self, there is some material presented here that has physical application.

1

NESTED SPIRITS

When sending earthbound spirits to the light, if there is difficulty in getting one of the spirits to leave, it is most likely a case of "nested spirits." The condition known as "nested spirits" is a condition in which there is a spirit possessed by another spirit. That spirit can in turn be possessed by another spirit etc. This may seem very strange but the explanation is very simple.

Our spirit fills our entire body. If we have another spirit present within us, it is not only within our body, it is within our spirit. If a person dies with such a spirit present, there is a possibility of that spirit staying within; thus a spirit can be possessed by another spirit. This can be repeated any number of times.

RELEASING NESTED SPIRITS

The following is a typical example of releasing nested spirits:

F.   "May I have permission to speak directly to the spirits that are present, using kinesiology?" (Test, yes).

"I am talking to the spirit that is present. There is darkness within you that is keeping you earthbound. Does

that darkness seem to have a personality of it's own?"
(Test, yes).

"That means that there is a second spirit hiding within the first one. I will call that spirit number two. Number two, you have darkness within you that keeps you earthbound. Does that darkness seem to have a personality of it's own?" (Test, yes).

"That means that there is a third spirit hiding within number two. I will call that spirit number three. Number three, you have darkness within you that keeps you earthbound. Does that darkness seem to have a personality of it's own?" (Test, yes).

"That means that there is a fourth spirit hiding within number three. I will call that spirit number four. Number four, you have darkness within you that keeps you earthbound. Does that darkness seem to have a personality of it's own?" (Test, no).

"Number four is the innermost spirit. Number four, have you ever had a body of your own?" (Test, no). "You have been hiding from Satan. He has never once rewarded you for anything. He always rules by fear. No matter how hard you try to please him, he punishes you and sets you up as a bad example. That is his way of keeping everyone in fear, and you hate it. Isn't that true?" (Test, yes).

"Number four, you don't have to be afraid of Satan any more. You have been controlled by him so long that you have forgotten who you are. You are literally a child of God. He is your Father, and Jesus Christ is your brother.

They both love you very much. They know that you were deceived, but they don't hold that against you. They are anxious for you to recognize the deception and return to them. All you need to do is turn to Christ. Call his name and say, 'I was deceived. Please forgive me. I want to come back.' They will welcome you back and you will once again become a being of light. You are free to go now. Please go to the light."

"I am now talking to number three. Number three, did that dark spirit within you go to the light?" (Test, yes).

"Number three, because that spirit is gone, now you can give your burdens to Christ and go to the light. Number two, you can do the same. Number one, you can also do the same."

"All of you, give your burdens to Christ then look up. You will see loved ones waiting to take you to a better place. You are now free to go. Please go to the light."

F.   "(Calling client by name), do you have any spirits of any kind hiding within you, connected to you, or in any way giving you input at this time?" (Test, no).

Note: Almost always, the innermost spirit will be a devil. I have always used the above logic and they go rather quickly. It is very obvious that Satan is a cruel master and his followers really do hate him. The ones like the one in this example are hiding from Satan.

2

REPATTERNING
Specific approach

The purpose of this procedure is to locate negative thought patterns that are affecting the client who is receiving the therapy, and then replace it with a corresponding positive thought pattern. The negative thought patterns affect our inner self. This manifests in many ways. It can greatly affect the mental and emotional stability of the individual. These negative thought patterns can also affect one's physical well being.

In this section I will first address the spiritual application of the principles being presented. This approach will allow the spirit to locate the negative thought patterns that one needs to release, and then replace them with the corresponding positive thought patterns.

Next there is a short presentation showing how to alter this approach so as to address specific physical problems.

There are a number of books on the market that have long lists of negative thought patterns followed by corresponding positive thought patterns. The one I use is in the little book "Heal Your Body," by Louise L. Hay. In her book she has three columns with the following headings: <u>Problem</u> (meaning physical problem), <u>Probable</u>

194

<u>Cause</u> (meaning the negative thought pattern associated with the physical problem), and <u>New Thought Pattern</u>.

SPIRITUAL APPLICATION

It is true that the negative thought patterns may have some real negative affects upon our body, often causing various illnesses; however, at this time I am not concerned with the physical problem. In this repatterning process I am only dealing with the two columns with the heading "Probable Cause" and "New Thought Pattern."

All statements, both the negative and the positive must be put into the first person. Sometimes the negative pattern listed under the "Probable Cause" column must be reworded to make it fit. For example: one of them is given as follows, "Family friction, arguments, child feeling unwelcome, in the way." I would reword this one as follows: "I am dealing with family friction and arguments. As a child I felt unwelcome and in the way."

PROCEDURE:

1. Do Brain Gym. (For details see page 214.)

2. Have the client hold one hand in front of his/her face with the palm of the hand facing toward the face. With the fingers of the other hand, tap the side of the hand between the wrist and the knuckle of the little finger. While

the client is doing this, with your finger draw a circle in front of the clients face, first rotating in one direction, then the other. The client will continue to tap the side of his/her hand and at the same time focus his/her eyes on your finger. While all of this is going on, simultaneously have the client repeat the affirmation found on the last page of the book, which is as follows:

I am a child of God. Everything I am and everything I do is a reflection of Him. Therefore, I choose to glorify God. I deserve a good life. I expect a good life. I claim a good life. I create a good life. I have a good life that glorifies God and demonstrates how a child of God should live.

Note: By having the client follow your finger with his/her eye while you draw a circle, the client will access different parts of the brain making the affirmation more effective.

3.   Find the negative thought patterns that are affecting the client. These are listed under the heading of "Probable Cause." This can be done very quickly by using kinesiology. It is not necessary to read every statement. You can just lay your hand over two open pages and do a kinesiology test. If any one issue is a problem, the spirit will indicate so by giving a weak test. You can then test each individual issue on the page. Record the negative patterns

by number, for example: Page 10 item 3.

4. Release each of the negative patterns and then immediately replace it with the corresponding positive affirmation. Do this one at a time.

Do this by stating the negative pattern and have the client repeat it after you. While doing this move your finger in a large sideways figure 8 pattern, in front of the client. At the same time have the client follow your finger with his/her eyes. Make sure that as you do this, your finger is moving in the direction that results in it going in an upward direction as you cross the midline. When the client has finished repeating the negative statement, he/she will say, "I give this to the Lord." At the same time he/she is saying, "I give this to the Lord," stop the figure 8 pattern. Gesture with that same hand, as if you are throwing the problem back away from both of you, giving it to the Lord.

Next while doing the same sideways figure 8 pattern, have the client repeat the corresponding positive affirmation. This time the client finishes by saying, "I accept." At the same time, stop the figure 8 pattern and then point your finger toward the client's heart.

To get more of the senses of the body involved and thus increase the effectiveness of the procedure, while repeating the positive affirmation have the client hold an essential oil in a position where it can be smelled. It doesn't matter which oil is used, but it is better if a different one is used for each affirmation.

5. Repeat Brain Gym as in step 1.

6. Ground the subject by dabbing a tiny bit of essential oil on each foot or ankle.

Note: The figure 8 pattern activates many different portions of the brain making the procedure more effective.

HEALING FROM PHYSICAL PROBLEMS.

In situations where the client is dealing with physical problems, this same approach can be used. Use the same six steps as given above except that instead of doing step 3 as given above, find the physical problem under the "problem" heading, and then make note of the associated negative thought pattern under the heading "Probable Cause." This negative thought pattern should then be released and replaced with the appropriate positive thought pattern by continuing with steps 4 through 6.

3

REPATTERNING
Generic Approach

The National Geographic magazine once had a very interesting article. It told of a factory that had a very loud disturbing noise. Experts were called in. They brought very sophisticated sound equipment to analyze the noise. They found that the noise had a very definite repeating pattern when printed out and viewed on a computer screen. The equipment was programmed to produce a noise with a pattern that was the exact opposite. When that new noise was created in the factory, the two noises completely cancelled out each other and the result was silence. The airline industry now uses this technology to protect the ears of the pilots. Using this same technology the pilot can wear earphones that produce a condition of silence.

The object of the following exercise is to apply this same principle to the healing and repatterning of one's old negative patterns. The Savior asked us to "cast our burdens upon Him." This is just one more tool, or procedure, to help you do exactly that.

In this repatterning exercise you will be concerned with negative energy patterns that you have acquired from three different sources: (1) Patterns inherited from your

199

ancestors, (2) Patterns which you brought with you from realms of existence prior to this earth life, and (3) Patterns you have acquired from the experiences of this lifetime.

Inasmuch as everything is energy (this goes without saying, but should be emphasized) the energy patterns we are dealing with include all thoughts, feelings, and emotions.

RELEASING OLD PATTERNS

Close your eyes and meditate. As you meditate, imagine that you have printed out on a screen an energy pattern that represents all the negative energy patterns that were passed on to you from your ancestors through your DNA. Once you get such an image in your mind, ask the Savior Jesus Christ to send his light and love to create a positive energy pattern that is the opposite. Let the new pattern cancel out then replace the old one.

People who are very visual will see the old patterns as negative chaotic patterns. They will then see them replaced with beautiful colorful patterns. If you are not visual just imagine the old and the new patterns. The process will still be effective.

After the period of meditation, finalize the process by raising the arm to the square and out loud say the following: (Note: You can change the words as long as the ideas are the same. It is best if you use your own words.)

200

"In the name of Jesus Christ, the only begotten son of the Father, I release all negative energy patterns which I have received from all sources, including my ancestors, my premortal existence, and my environment. I ask the Lord to send his light and love to cancel them out and replace them with the corresponding positive energy patterns. I accept this healing with praise, love, and gratitude. Accept. Accept. Accept. Forever with me."

As you say, "Accept. Accept. Accept." Tap the middle of your chest about two inches below the collarbone. As you say, "Forever with me," hold the palm of your hand over the navel.

4

CORRECTION FOR LIMITING HUMAN PROGRAMMING

Every experience of your life is recorded in your permanent long-term memory. All of these memories are compared to each other in such a way as to create your perception of reality. This perception of reality determines how you react to the day-to-day situations of life.

For example: You may have had many experiences that programmed you to be fearful. Such human programming can seriously limit your success in many aspects of life.

The purpose of this exercise is to find the limiting human programming and eliminate it.

Ask your inner-self the question: **What human programming limits me from knowing I am holy and completely divine?**

Make sure you are asking your heart, not your mind. You may have to meditate and ponder for a few minutes. If given time, your inner-self will give you the answer. When the answer comes, you will feel it in your heart. Don't try to rush the process. The answer may be just a word such as fear, doubt, anger, or control. It might be a phrase such as low self-esteem.

So that you can measure the degree of success, by using kinesiology measure on a scale of zero to ten the degree to which you are limited by this human programming.

Give the limiting human programming to the Lord. It may help to visualize that programming as a dark negative energy, which can be eliminated and given away. One way to do this is to take several deep breaths. As you inhale imagine that you are inhaling light. As you exhale imagine that you are exhaling the darkness associated with that limiting human programming.

Test again, on a scale of zero to ten, the degree to which you are limited. This will help you determine the effectiveness of what you have done. If the test reveals a level other than zero, repeat the process of giving the programming to the Lord.

Later more negative human programming may surface and the treatment can be repeated.

The process can be repeated using other questions. Some other questions that can be asked are as follows:

What human programming limits me from the abundance the universe wants me to have?

What human programming limits me from knowing basic eternal truths?

5

EFT TAPPING SEQUENCE

The following is often referred to as "EFT" meaning "Emotion Freedom Technique." The technique is really an acupressure approach to dealing with stress, addictions, phobias and other hang-ups. This is an extension to the procedure given in my first book for overcoming fears and phobias and is ideal for some difficult cases. As one goes through a session for the healing of the inner self, it should be kept in mind that the issues one is dealing with are also recorded in the physical self. This tapping sequence, if used at the end of the session, is a good way to release those issues from the physical self.

Begin by having the subject do "Brain Gym" as described in the appendage.

Have the subject hold one hand with the palm of the hand facing toward the face. With the fingers of the other hand tap the side of the hand between the wrist and the knuckle of the little finger. While doing this, have the subject focus their eyes on your finger. With your finger slowly draw a circle in front of the subject's face, first one direction then the other. While all of this is going on simultaneously, have the subject repeat the following affirmation:

"I am a child of God. Everything I am and everything I do is a reflection of Him. Therefore, I choose to glorify God. I deserve a good life. I expect a good life. I claim a good life. I create a good life. I have a good life which glorifies God and demonstrates how a child of God should live."

Next have the person you are helping imitate you as you tap the following points on your own body. Both sides of the body should be tapped at the same time when possible. Each point should be tapped seven times, rapidly and gently.

The end of each eyebrow next to the nose

The bone at the outside corner of the eye

The middle of the upper lip under the nose

The middle of the lower lip

The cheekbone directly below the center of the eye

The collarbone near the neck

The ribs just under the armpits

The little fingernail

The cheekbone again

The collar bone again

The side at the base of the rib cage

The middle fingernail

The index fingernail

The thumbnail

The back of the hand between the bones that connect to the knuckles of the little finger and the ring finger, about 3/4 inch from both knuckles.

End by doing "Brain Gym" again.

Note: When finished, test the stress level on a scale from zero to ten. If the test at the end gives anything other than zero, have the client tap four toenails all at the same time, using two fingers of each hand. The toes to be tapped are the big toes and the ones next to them. This time tap twenty-one times.

There is no magic in the numbers seven and twenty one. I suggest those numbers because they work. If you tap a few more time, it really won't matter.

6

SATANIC RITUAL
MULTILAYERED PROGRAMMING

As stated in my first book, one of the effects of satanic ritual is to program you to respond, when triggered, in a predetermined way. In effect you become a human robot. To prevent one from healing from the effects of ritual, the victims are often programmed on many different levels. In other words, the programming is multi-layered. Thus, as one goes through therapy, the therapist may think that the programming has been released or canceled out, but in reality only one layer of programming has been dealt with. Finding all layers of programming and releasing it can therefore become a very tedious process.

Greek letters such as alpha, beta, delta, gamma, theta, and omega usually designate these different layers of programming. Each layer of programming can be accessed with its own trigger.

In addition to the multi-layered programming there are multi-layered implants. These implants act as if you had many dark spiritual computers within you, each with its own unique programs and each with its own trigger to access it. These "spiritual computers" are designated by the six different basic colors plus black and white.

207

We are taught in scripture that God knows all things from the beginning. In other words, before you were born God knew every trial that would befall you, including every bit of satanic ritual and the associated programming. The technique I will present here, to be used to help one heal from satanic ritual, is based on the assumption that God is a loving Father, and that He sent us to earth with a built-in healing mechanism or program that is designed to heal us and release all the effects of ritual from all levels.

As I work with a victim of satanic ritual I test to find the extent of the ritual, including how much multi-layered programming and multi-layered spiritual computers are present. It is important that the victim's spirit be alerted to the extent of the ritual so that all the effects of ritual can be addressed in the healing process.

I have the client raise his/her arm to the square and repeat after me. **"In the name of Jesus Christ I petition my Heavenly Father. Please activate the healing program within me, healing me on all levels, removing effect of satanic ritual.**

In the name of Jesus Christ I command that all effects of satanic ritual be null and void. I command that all programs and their back-ups on all levels be canceled and deleted. I dismiss all effects of satanic ritual and cancel them out along with every spirit, thought form, energy, program, and residue associated with them. Cancel, cancel, cancel, and forever cancel."

The client taps his/her chest in the middle about two inches below his/her collarbone while he/she says cancel, then holds the navel with the palm of his/her hand while saying forever cancel.

The client again raises his/her arm to the square and repeats after me. **"In the name of Jesus Christ I petition my Heavenly Father. Please send heavenly surgeons from the realm of light to surgically remove every implant, weapon, tool, and shunt, including every spiritual computer on every level. I ask those heavenly surgeons to immediately heal the wounds that are left in my spirit. I accept this healing with praise, love and gratitude. Accept, accept, accept, forever with me."** Again the client taps the thymus and holds the navel.

Always finish the process by filling the void that has been created by the above procedure. Have the client again raise his/her arm to the square and repeat the following prayer. **"In the name of Jesus Christ I petition my Heavenly Father. Please fill the void within me by giving me at this time every positive spirit gift, intelligence, light, and anything else that I need to help me accomplish my life's mission."**

Note: It is not necessary to use my exact words but

the thoughts expressed should be the same. Some people feel that they can't do the work until they have all the "correct words" memorized. <u>There is no magic in the words. It is the thought that counts.</u>

SECTION FOUR

APPENDAGE

The following are some summaries and suggestions for your convenience. It is important to note that these are only suggestions. You may want to make changes to fit your personality. It is also important to note that exact wording is not important. Please do not tie yourself to an exact script; allow some flexibility so that the Holy Spirit can more easily work through you.

HEALING THE INNER SELF
SUGGESTED SEQUENCE

1.   Make sure the lie detector works. (Introduce Kinesiology.)

2.   Test for switching.

3.   Test each chakra making sure each one is open and flowing properly.

4.   Test for spirit attachments. If present, send them to the light.

5.   Test for spirits that may have come at the time of birth. If present, send them to the light and fill the void.

6.   Measure the stress level.

7.   Do an age regression to find issues from the past. Release the issue. Repeat until no more issues from the past are found.

8.   Test for issues related to father, mother, brother, sister, extended family, neighbors, etc. Release when found.

9.   Test for issues related to fear, anger, abuse, rejection, etc. Release when found.

10.   Test for negative spiritual gifts. Release when found, then fill the void.

11.   Test for fragmentation of the spirit involving fragments large enough to have a personality of their own. Do soul retrieval if needed.

12.   Test for fragmentation of the spirit involving small fragments without a personality of their own. Retrieve them if needed.

13.   Release fears and phobias as needed.

14.   Test for ritual abuse. Release as needed.

15   Release the negative programming from the physical self.

BRAIN GYM

The purpose of this exercise is to balance the energies in the two hemispheres of the brain

Cross your legs at the ankle. Now extend your arms with the thumbs pointing down. Cross the one hand over the other and interlock the fingers. Now rotate the arms down, around, and up, so as to have your hands and arms against your chest. Now take three deep breaths. When finished uncross the arms and legs.

Using a finger hold one nostril closed while inhaling through the other nostril. Then move your finger to the other side and exhale. Without changing your finger inhale, and then switch to the other nostril to exhale. In other words, inhale through the left nostril, exhale through the right, then inhale through the right and exhale through the left.

EFT TAPPING SEQUENCE

1. Begin by having the subject do "Brain Gym."

2. While drawing a circle in front of the client's face have the client focus his/her eyes on your finger and repeat the "I Am A Child Of God" affirmation (last page of the book) and at the same time tap the side of his/her hand.

3. The client will tap each of the following points seven times:

The end of each eyebrow next to the nose

The bone at the outside corner of the eye

The middle of the upper lip under the nose

The middle of the lower lip

The cheekbone directly below the center of the eye

The collarbone near the neck

The ribs just under the armpits

The little fingernail

The cheekbone again

The collar bone again

The side at the base of the rib cage

The middle fingernail

The index fingernail

The thumbnail

The back of the hand between the bones that connect to the knuckles of the little finger and the ring finger, about 3/4 inch from both knuckles.

4. Again do "Brain Gym."

CASTING OUT DEVILS

Mark 16:16-18

16. He that believeth and is baptized shall be saved; but he that believeth not shall be damned.

17. And these signs shall follow them that believe; In my name shall they cast out devils; they shall speak with new tongues;

18. They shall take up serpents; and if they drink any deadly thing, it shall not hurt them: they shall lay hands on the sick, and they shall recover.

Doctrine and Covenants 84:64-68

64. Therefore, as I said unto mine apostles I say unto you again, that every soul who believeth on your words, and is baptized by water for the remission of sins, shall receive the Holy Ghost.

65. And these signs shall follow them that believe—

66. In my name they shall do many wonderful works;

67. In my name they shall cast out devils;

68. In my name they shall heal the sick;

Journal of Discourses Vol. 4 Page 133

This is a quotation of Brigham Young speaking at

the funeral of Jedediah M. Grant.

You never felt a pain and ache, or felt disagreeable, or uncomfortable in your bodies and minds, but what an evil spirit was present causing it. Do you realize that the ague, the fever, the chills, the severe pain in the head, the pleurisy, or any pain in the system from the crown of the head to the soles of the feet is put there by the devil? You don't realize this, do you?

I say but little about this matter, because I do not want you to realize it. When you have the rheumatism, do you realize that the devil put that upon you? No, but you say, "I got wet, caught cold, and thereby got the rheumatism."

Note: Brigham Young may have been a little too strong. He may be right but I would not say it that way. I would say that the evil spirits sometimes cause the problems; at other times they contribute to the problem. It seems as if the illness or pain weakens one's energy field. This allows the spirits to enter. Once they are there, they aggravate and compound the problem.

LOGIC TO BE USED WITH DEVILS

1. You were deceived by Satan and he has confused your mind to the point that you don't even remember who you are. You are a child of God and Jesus Christ is your brother. They both love you and are anxious for you to return to them. They know that you were deceived but they do not hold that against you. All they ask is that you call out to them and say, "I was deceived. Please forgive me. I want to come back and be with you."

2. There is a law which guarantees that there is opposition in all things. You have been fighting against Christ for millions of years. In this fight, you have been leading people away from Christ causing them to follow Satan. The law of opposition guarantees that if someone can leave Christ and follow Satan, you can leave Satan and go to Christ.

3. Many of the devils are afraid that if they go to Christ He will punish them for having fought against Him for so long. I counter this by telling them: In any war, right up until the last day of battle, some warrior will wake up one morning and say, "I have been fighting for the wrong cause." And they defect. When they go over to the other side they are not punished. They are welcomed and invited to join with them in battle. So it is with Christ. He will welcome you with open arms.

4. Satan has told his followers that because they chose to go with him they are now subjected to eternal damnation and are therefore stuck with him forever and can do nothing about it. Satan is very good at quoting scripture, and he does it often to suit his purposes; but he never quotes D. & C. 19:6-12 There the Lord explains that Eternal punishment is God's punishment, and Endless punishment is God's punishment because Eternal and Endless are two of God's names; but it can come to an end.

5. Satan has told them to avoid the light, and that the light will kill them. Bless them with light and let them feel how good it is.

6. All that is necessary for one to be released from the bondage of Satan is to turn to Christ and say, "Lord, have mercy on me. I was deceived. Please forgive me and let me come back." The Lord Jesus Christ will welcome them back with open arms.

7. If the spirit still does not believe you, tell it "Christ is a God of truth and cannot lie. If you look up seeking Christ, He will be there. Ask Him if all I have told you is true. He will verify the truth and you will know that deliverance is available."

LOGIC TO BE USED WITH UNCLEAN SPIRITS

You are a child of God. As such you are part of the God race and you were created with power to create. Your power to create is much greater than you would ever imagine. This is the way it works, what you think about with emotion you create.

We mortals do not usually make the connection between our thoughts and the events in our lives because all the things that we create are first created spiritually then physically. There is usually a time lag between our thoughts and when they manifest in our life. If I have a negative thought combined with a negative emotion it creates a negative thought-form, which exists in the spirit realm. It may take considerable time before it manifests in the physical realm.

In your realm there is no time lag. What you think about is immediately created in that spiritual realm where you reside. Your negative thoughts and emotions create negative thought-forms that are immediately in the spiritual realm where you reside. As a result, you are creating a never-ending nightmare of the worst events of your life. You are trapping yourself in hell. What you think about, you create.

Christ has said, "Cast your burdens upon me. I will suffer for you and you will not have to suffer any more."

If you will turn to Christ and say, "Lord, please take away my guilt, my sorrow, my grief, my anger, or what ever negative thought and emotion that is troubling you, He will take that negative burden from you and replace it with exquisite light, peace, and love. Then, when you look up, you will see loved ones and friends waiting to take you into a better place, a place called paradise.

You can go now. Please give your burdens to Christ and go to the light.

ELIMINATING NEGATIVE SPIRITUAL GIFTS.

While holding the arm to the square repeat the following: **"In the name of Jesus Christ I command that all negative spiritual gifts depart. I dismiss them without argument and cancel them out, along with every spirit, thought form, energy, and residue associated with them. Cancel, (tap). Cancel, (tap). Cancel, (tap). Forever cancel."**

While saying, "cancel," tap the chest over the thymus, which is in the middle of the chest about two inches below the collarbone. While saying, "Forever cancel," hold the navel with the palm of one hand.

Note: Exact wording is not important. Change the wording to fit your personality. It is the meaning and intent that makes this effective.

FILLING THE VOID

When all spirits have been sent away, or when all negative spiritual gifts have been eliminated, there is a void that must be filled.

The Orientals who have studied spiritual energy for two thousand years have found that when one raises their arm to the square, as when one takes an oath, the arm acts as an antenna to draw spiritual energy, increasing and magnifying the power of the spoken words. When filling the void we need that extra spiritual energy. The client raises the arm to the square and repeats the following:

"In the name of Jesus Christ I petition my Heavenly Father. Please fill the void within me by giving me at this time every positive spirit gift, intelligence, light, and anything else that I need to help me accomplish my life's mission."

The above is followed by having the client tap his/her chest in the middle about two inches below your collarbone while saying "accept, (tap), accept, (tap), accept, (tap)", then hold the navel with the palm of the hand and say, "forever with me."

Note: Exact wording is not important. Change the wording to fit your personality. It is the meaning and intent that makes this effective.

RELEASING SATANIC RITUAL

As I work with a victim of satanic ritual, I test to find the extent of the ritual, including how much multi-layered programming, and multi-layer spiritual computers are present. It is important that the victim's spirit is alerted to the extent of the ritual so that all the effects of ritual can be addressed in the healing process.

I have the client raise his/her arm to the square and repeat after me. **"In the name of Jesus Christ, I petition my Heavenly Father. Please activate the healing program within me, healing me on all levels, removing all effect of satanic ritual.**

In the name of Jesus Christ I command that all effects of curses, hexes, spells, voodoo or any other form of satanic ritual be null and void. I dismiss it and cancel it out from every aspect of my being, including my physical nature, my spirit, my mind, my intellect, my energy fields, my memory and my DNA. I command that all programs and their back-ups on all levels be canceled and deleted. I dismiss all effects of satanic ritual and cancel them out, along with every spirit, thought form, energy, program, and residue associated with them. Cancel, cancel, cancel, forever cancel. A-men."

The client taps his/her chest in the middle about

two inches below his/her collarbone while he/she says cancel, then holds the navel with the palm of his/her hand while saying forever cancel.

The client again raises his/her arm to the square and repeats after me. **"In the name of Jesus Christ I petition my Heavenly Father, please send heavenly surgeons from the realm of light to surgically remove every implant, weapon, tool, and shunt, including every spiritual computer on every level. I ask those heavenly surgeons to immediately heal the wounds that are left in my spirit. I accept this healing with praise, love and gratitude. Accept, accept, accept, forever with me."** Again the client taps the thymus and holds the navel.

Note: Exact wording is not important. Change the wording to fit your personality. It is the meaning and intent that makes this effective.

PRAYER FOR PROTECTION

We all have an energy field around that acts as our shield of protection. The negative daily experiences tend to ware it away. We need to renew it every day. This can be done with the following prayer.

Heavenly Father, please place your light and love around me, every member of my family, and everything we own. Please let that light become a perfect shield of protection to protect us from all harm, evil and evil influences whether it comes from man, nature or the world of spirit.

I am a child of God.

Everything I am and everything I do is a reflection of Him.

Therefore, I choose to glorify God.

I deserve a good life.

I expect a good life.

I claim a good life.

I create a good life.

I have a good life that glorifies God and demonstrates how a child of God should live.